.

"The gap between wanting to spend time with Jesus and merely logging time with him comes down to imagination. In *Friendship with Jesus*, Dan Heavenor helps us close that gap. Walking us through an ancient approach to prayer and weaving into it his own story of learning to be a friend of Jesus, he guides us to a place of freedom and delight. If you, like me, want a richer, fuller, more fruitful prayer life, the answer, literally, is in your hands."

—Mark Buchanan, author of *God Walk: Moving at the Speed of Your Soul*

"In *Friendship with Jesus*, master spiritual director, Dan Heavenor, guides you through immersive meditations into the ancient world of Palestine and helps you to see Jesus with new eyes—as if for the very first time. You will hear Jesus calling you by name and awaken to the sheer wonder of being his beloved."

—Ken Shigematsu, pastor and author of *God in My Everything.*

"Dan Heavenor gives the reader a fresh and inviting way to engage with the companion of our soul. *Friendship with Jesus* draws us in, takes us deeper, moves us further, as we set our sights on reinvigorating this loving union with the one who travels with us on our journey of life."

—Joyce Rupp, author of *Jesus, Guide of My Life:*
Reflections for the Lenten Journey

"*Friendship with Jesus* truly cultivates friendship with Jesus! Dan Heavenor is a skillful guide on a journey of deepening acquaintance with the one about whom we are apt to speak and think—and even desire to know—yet, too often, ineffectively befriend. The good news is that there are means of grace we can practice in our friendship with Jesus, and this book immerses the receptive reader into those ways of imaginative and contemplative prayer."

—Susan Phillips, author of *Candlelight:*
Illuminating the Art of Spiritual Direction

"Dan Heavenor's book is a gentle, captivating, and profound journey into friendship with Jesus through imaginative prayer. I grew up singing 'What a Friend We Have in Jesus,' but apart from warm and fuzzy feelings while we sang, I didn't know what friendship with Jesus could be. I wish we'd had this book back then. I'm glad we have it now. The many stories that Dan tells, and the guided prayer that he invites us into, make an ancient practice fresh and life-giving for today."

—Jonathan R. Wilson, Senior Consultant for Theological Integration,
Canadian Baptist Ministries

"In a secular age, one seemingly devoid of divine action, prayer can seem both useless and wasteful of time. If you are ready and longing to break free from this stifling secularism, read this book. Dan Heavenor invites us into a contemplative, receptive, and imaginative way of praying that opens our eyes to the ways that Jesus is indeed at work in our lives and our world."

—Tim Dickau, author of *Forming Christian Communities in a Secular Age: Recovering Humility and Hope*

"'Over the two decades I have known Dan Heavenor, I have listened to him 'talk out' his understanding of the dynamics of actually enjoying knowing Jesus as a real person in real life. I have watched him then take others through the process of cultivating a 'lived experience' of Jesus of Nazareth through praying with the imagination. So, I am very glad Dan has finally written this book! Read the introduction, the first exercise, and you will find yourself engaged in a new level of interaction and intimacy with the living Jesus."

—Darrell Johnson, author of *Experiencing the Trinity: Living in the Relationship at the Center of the Universe*

"In *Friendship with Jesus*, Dan Heavenor encourages us in the ancient practice of placing the God-given gift of our imagination at the service of our faith. He helps us to see that by imaginatively entering the gospel stories we can encounter the living Christ with both mind and heart. This book will be a gift to all who desire to know, love, and follow Jesus more deeply."

—Trevor Hudson, author of *Seeking God: Finding Another Kind of Life with St. Ignatius and Dallas Willard*

"Dan Heavenor is a trustworthy guide to this journey into prayer as a deepening experience of friendship with Jesus. This book is thoughtful, honest, and practical. It doesn't just talk about prayer. It shows you how to pray and helps you along. And it keeps your eyes on Jesus all the way."

—Bruce Hindmarsh, Professor of Spiritual Theology, Regent College

"In *Friendship with Jesus*, Dan Heavenor offers an irresistibly disarming, warm-hearted, imminently practical guide to imaginative prayer as an essential pathway to intimacy with Jesus. This is a book that I've been searching for, one I will confidently give to anyone—from the curious seeker to the mature believer—who longs for a deeper experience of God's love."

—Carolyn Arends, Director of Education, Renovaré

Friendship with Jesus

Friendship with Jesus

An Imaginative Prayer Journey

DAN HEAVENOR

WIPF & STOCK · Eugene, Oregon

FRIENDSHIP WITH JESUS
An Imaginative Prayer Journey

Wipf & Stock
An Imprint of Wipf and Stock Publishers
199 W. 8th Ave., Suite 3
Eugene, OR 97401

www.wipfandstock.com

PAPERBACK ISBN: 979-8-3852-1291-0
HARDCOVER ISBN: 979-8-3852-1292-7
EBOOK ISBN: 979-8-3852-1293-4

NIV

The Message

Dedication
For Andrea

Contents

Acknowledgements ix
Introduction xi

PART I *Preparing for the Journey*

1 The Prayer Journey 3

2 Engaging Our Imagination in Prayer   17

3 The Practice Run 27

PART II *The Journey of Friendship*

4 Watching Jesus 39

5 Meeting Jesus 50

6 Following Jesus 65

7 Trusting Jesus 77

8 Surrendering to Jesus 92

9 Dying with Jesus 107

10 Rising with Jesus 120

Epilogue Coming Home to Jesus 133
Bibliography 141

Acknowledgements

THIS BOOK HAS TAKEN me a long time to write. I began thinking seriously about what it meant to have a friendship with Jesus over twenty-five years ago and since then, many people have walked with me, challenged me, loved me, and encouraged me to keep going, to keep pressing in, and to write about it. I have also had many people ask me to accompany them on their journey. I would not be the same person without all these friends, and my gratitude is difficult to put into words. I want to particularly name the men who have opened up their lives to me and have been precious soul-friends to me, some for a season, some for many seasons. They opened their hearts to me and allowed me to open mine to them, cultivating and nurturing the ground of friendship. They are Tim Willson, Dave Sotropa, Shaun Marshall, Rob Snair, Cam Roxburgh, Dave Ward, and Jeff Hayashi. These last two I want to especially acknowledge. Dave Ward, author, professor, and dear friend saw me as an author, and called me so long before I believed it myself. Jeff Hayashi, lifelong friend and fellow sojourner, has listened to me for many hours as I grappled and struggled with these themes. These men have loved me well and I am a better person because of their friendship. Ann Thakkar, another dear friend, read an early draft and helped me find my voice. Karen Hollenbeck-Wuest read an early draft, challenged me to write the book I actually wanted to write, and then brought her editing skills to bear. It is a far better book because of her time, patience, and skill (the deficits are all mine). And Jeff Schuliger took on a late draft that I believed was finished and made it much better. There are many others who have contributed to this book through their willingness to take the journey of prayer themselves as well as walk with me as friends. I am grateful for them all.

My kids, Hannah, Cass, Tori, and Michael (that order is for Hannah) have each in their own way contributed to this book, mostly by loving me beyond what I deserve as their Dad. They heard for many years that Dad was writing a book but, I'm sure, often doubted if it would ever actually exist. Well, here it is!

And finally, but most importantly, my wife Andrea, the love of my life, who has loved me, encouraged me, and patiently waited for me as I slowly brought this book into existence. I would not know Jesus like I do if not for her. She is my greatest gift.

Introduction

PRAYER WAS SOMETHING I was introduced to early in life. In our Christian home, we prayed a lot. We prayed for our food. We prayed after family devotions. We listened to prayer in church. The older I got, the more I received the message that prayer was something I should be doing on my own. It was how I was supposed to talk to God. The problem was, I had no idea how to pray. Oh, I could string a few sentences together, mimicking the tone and themes of prayers I had heard for thankfulness, help, protection, and provision, but it mostly fell flat with me. Because God was not very real to me, I found it hard to distinguish between praying and thinking. Prayer was a topic to think about (and feel guilty about) rather than an avenue for a relationship.

If prayer was meant to be communication between me and God, then it seemed to me that one of the parties hadn't shown up. Most of my prayers felt as if I was talking to myself, the words coming out of my mind and crashing to the floor. When I prayed, I often felt like I was picking up a phone to have a conversation and hearing only static, or deathly silence, on the other end. Why would I continue doing that? The longing for connection, and the guilt, would keep me coming back but I grew more and more frustrated with my experience of prayer. This went on for years. I never seriously doubted God's existence but I struggled with the *reality* of God in my life.

The truth of Jesus' presence and love was part of the believing package of being a Christian but my lived experience of that presence and love was sporadic at best. I had been taught that if I believed then God would be present in my life, but since that did not seem real, prayer seemed pointless. However, I continued to find myself drawn to the notion of having a *relationship* with God, a concept that was often used in my Christian circles. Supposedly, we all had a relationship with God, and yet I knew this was not true of me. Everywhere I looked in the Bible, God seemed to be talking to people, listening to people, conversing with people, forging deep and real relationships. In my experience, God was a mere acquaintance—at best.

One day I was reading through a few chapters of the Gospel of John when I came upon the passage in John 15 where Jesus calls his disciples *friends*. "I no longer call you servants . . . Instead I have called you friends" (John 15:15). I had read this many times before but this time it seemed particularly striking. This idea of being a friend of Jesus began to burrow its way into my soul, but the more I thought about it the more confused and angry I became. It simply seemed impossible. While I ached for a real relationship with Jesus, I feared that my usual experience of God's absence and my spiritual emptiness would never end and I would inevitably realize that my longing to intimately know God was a grand delusion. For years I had longed to have a real relationship with God. I would hear other people talk about hearing God speak to them and I would feel a mixture of longing and skepticism. Were they making this up? Was there something wrong with me? Would I ever have such an intimate connection with Jesus?

I felt as if I were coming to a crossroads. There was no escape from Jesus' invitation to become his friend. It was right there in Scripture! But, if I accepted his invitation, it would mean that I would have to relate to him as an actual person, a person I could talk to, listen to, and spend time with. I have been blessed with tremendous friends in my life. I know what a friendship is. Friends are there. Friends are real. Friends care about us and listen to us. I do not have to guess what my friend might say to me. This is what I deeply longed for with Jesus. I could no longer ignore my deep desire to have a real friendship with Jesus. I felt I could not go on without it but I had no idea how it might come about. It did not seem that Jesus met any of these criteria for friendship that I knew so well with my actual friends.

At that time I was working split shifts as a bus driver and I was struggling with all these questions and feelings as I drove. As I walked home one day from my morning shift, I was feeling angry at Jesus for making this promise of friendship and then withholding it from me. Though it was a beautiful sunny summer morning, the weather did not reflect my mood. I felt exhausted by all the mental gymnastics I had gone through to try to make this promise seem true in my life. I obviously had no friendship with Jesus.

My heart was pounding as I walked. Eventually, it all spilled out.

"You call yourself a friend?" I yelled, shaking my fist at the cloudless sky, not caring who heard me. "My friends *talk* to me!"

I stopped. I was physically shaking.

"Why won't you talk to me?" I said, this time in defeat. I was done.

Immediately, I sensed what I can only describe as a Presence.

"Dan, I talk to you all the time."

I fell to the ground weeping. I knew it was the Lord. I lay on the ground weeping for several minutes, not knowing how to respond.

After that encounter on the roadside, my heart began to soften, and my anger subsided. Even though all my questions were not answered my posture toward God began to shift.

ENTERING A FRIENDSHIP

While prayer was still difficult for me I slowly began to realize that I simply *had* to pray if I hoped for any kind of relationship with Jesus. My spiritual life depended on it. Over time, I began to pray because I didn't want God to fade into the background of my life. I prayed because I wanted to have a real friendship with Jesus. In my own spiritual healing, as I have discovered the gift of imaginative prayer, I no longer see prayer as a skill to improve or a discipline that I practice out of guilt. Now prayer is how I get together for a meal and conversation with my friend Jesus.

Prayer has slowly become a gift, a way of being with Jesus that sustains me and gives me hope. Through imaginative prayer especially, God has become a *reality* in my life. As I read the Gospels, imagining myself on those streets and in those homes watching and listening to Jesus my aching heart is quenched. I hear again and again, "I have called you friend" (John 15:15).

Back in the sixteenth century, Ignatius of Loyola popularized this way of praying with the imagination. It has come to be known as "Ignatian contemplation." His *Spiritual Exercises* have been a rich resource for thousands of people who desire to pray and grow closer to Jesus. He took guidance from many who had gone before him, encouraging people to enter into the stories in the Gospels as a way to experience the reality of Jesus, so that they would fall in love with him as a friend and fully devote their lives to serving him as their Lord.

As I engaged with imaginative prayer, Jesus became more real to me and our relationship began to develop. As I watched and listened to Jesus, I discovered that many of the relational dynamics in my other friendships found a parallel in my emerging friendship with Jesus. This realization helped me slow down and allow the friendship to develop more naturally. I stopped worrying about what I *believed* and simply began to pay attention to Jesus and imagine that I was meeting with him as a real person. I felt free to wait for Jesus to offer his friendship to me afresh.

When I lead others in imaginative prayer I have seen friendship with Jesus develop and flourish in people as they begin with a posture of a curious onlooker, then an intrigued questioner, then a nervous but excited follower, and finally a committed disciple and friend. This is the path that Jesus' first friends walked. After they met Jesus, they began to follow him, and slowly developed a friendship with him. When we read and pray the Gospels we can walk along a similar path as we follow the way of Jesus.

Part I (chapters 1–3) of this book prepares us for the imaginative prayer journey. On any journey, there are some things we need to know ahead of time, such as where we are going, how we will get there, and what we can expect along the way. Part II (chapters 4–10) outlines the journey itself, investigating the distinct "stages" of friendship as they often emerge when we encounter Jesus in imaginative prayer. I identify these stages as watching Jesus, meeting Jesus, following Jesus, trusting Jesus, surrendering to Jesus, dying with Jesus, and rising with Jesus. I conclude with an epilogue about coming home to Jesus. Though there is an intentional sequence in the ordering of these chapters, living with Jesus, as with any other person, does not lend itself to a linear analysis. We move in and out of these stages, stumbling forward, circling back, but always growing and going somewhere. Each chapter reflects upon these stages as they are revealed through Jesus' interactions with his friends in the Gospels, how we might experience these stages with our own friends and how these stages might play out in our lives as we live them with Jesus. These stages are not achievements that we are trying to accomplish. Rather, we simply allow ourselves to be drawn into the story and led by our new friend Jesus, who includes us as his friends.

As you journey though each stage, I hope you will discover how praying with your imagination can open up a new awareness of Jesus and deepen your love for him as you grow in friendship. To help you with this, I have included imaginative prayer exercises in each chapter that invite you into scenes from Jesus' life. Read the story in scripture, then enter into the scene prayerfully using the text provided in the exercise, listening for Jesus' invitation into friendship. (Audio versions of these exercises can be found at www.danheavenor.com)

The journey of imaginative prayer is a process, a way of life, a way of becoming who we are created to be as image bearers of God who are being transformed through our union with Christ. We pray Jesus' life so that it will become our life! This way of praying has opened a deeper friendship with Jesus in my own life and so I invite you to join me in your own journey of friendship with Jesus. As I share what I and others have experienced with Jesus through imaginative prayer I hope you will be able to enter in and receive what Jesus has for you.

PART I

Preparing for the Journey

Before we embark on any journey, we need to decide the nature of our trip. Will we go on a cruise to Alaska? To a fishing lodge in Northern Canada? Camping along the Pacific Coast? Sailing among the Queen Charlotte islands? Once we decide on a destination, we need to make the appropriate preparations.

In this book, we are embarking on a prayer journey of friendship. Before we venture out we need to understand the nature of the landscape we will traverse and so in chapter 1 I will discuss the best posture for this journey of imaginative prayer, a posture of listening and noticing. We also need to pack some equipment for the road ahead and so chapter 2 will discuss the main piece of equipment we will use, our imagination, and how it might serve us on our journey. Finally, chapter 3 will discuss how to use this equipment of our imagination on our particular prayer journey.

CHAPTER 1

The Prayer Journey

More than anything, prayer is primarily listening and waiting.[1]
—Henri Nouwen

One day Jesus was praying in a certain place.
When he finished, one of his disciples said to him,
"Lord, teach us to pray."

—Luke 11:1

WHEN WE WERE IN our early twenties, my friend Tim and I decided to take a few months off from college to travel. We had lots of ideas. Would we backpack around Europe? Would we sign up to work on a tall ship? We finally settled on cycling around Australia. We wanted the freedom that cycling offered and since our trip was planned during the fall and winter in Canada, we wanted Australia's summer weather—and waves for surfing! To prepare for our trip we applied for passports and visas and bought bikes and backpacks along with large containers for carrying fresh water through the hot, desert regions of Australia. We researched the country—a little—to know where we should go and discover the things we did not want to miss. Eventually, we purchased our airline tickets, making sure they allowed for multiple stops in case the cycling got too onerous and we needed to hop a

1. Nouwen, *Spiritual Direction*, 63.

flight to the next city. Finally, as the fall rains settled over Vancouver, we made the final preparations with a strong sense of adventure, eager for the journey ahead.

The journey of this book, rather than a vacation trip, is a journey of prayer. And rather than Australia, our destination is the New Testament Gospels. Like traveling, prayer is an activity that many of us know well. We may have been doing it since we were children. Tim and I had traveled before. Both of us had been on many family vacations and trips of different kinds and knew what traveling required but this trip to Australia was much longer than we were used to and had some unique features to prepare for. Our prayer journey also has some unique features to it and, therefore, requires some particular preparations before we venture out. Though prayer is a common practice for many of us, imaginative prayer may be new to you. It has some unique qualities to it and so this chapter will unpack and reflect on this kind of prayer before we head out on our journey.

"TEACH US TO PRAY"

Though we may have been praying for many years and desiring to pray well, we can find praying a struggle. Prayer often stirs up feelings of both guilt and longing, Though our hearts may cry, "If only I could pray better," we so often find ourselves captive to the distractions of our age—the internet, computer, phone, television. These external distractions are accompanied by many internal ones—our anxious hearts, relational difficulties, financial worries—and so it can be difficult to find the time or energy for prayer. But if we pay attention to the undercurrents of longing beneath all the noise, if we allow ourselves even a moment of quiet, we may see a faint light flickering in the darkness, beckoning us to follow the pathway of prayer, which will lead us to a homecoming with our Creator.

In Luke's Gospel, Jesus' friends approached him one day and asked, "Teach us to pray." I wonder what prompted this question? As faithful Jews, the disciples would have been well-versed in prayer. What had they noticed about the way Jesus prayed? Could they sense the intimacy Jesus enjoyed with his father? Did they notice that his way of prayer was quite different from theirs?

When we find ourselves desiring to pray, we are responding to a stirring of the Spirit deep within our hearts. When God draws near to us, our hearts respond with the longing to connect to God. But we often get in the way. We ask Jesus to teach us to pray, and then we become distracted and do not listen to his response.

My prayer life stumbled along sporadically for many years. While I sometimes longed for more, it wasn't until my life was in crisis and I began to articulate my longing for more of God, that I found myself being ushered into a new experience of prayer. My spiritual director pointed out to me one day that my desire for prayer was actually a desire for God and my desire and longing for God *was* the presence of God within me. This revelation came at a time when I was wondering if God was present in my life at all. My longing for God, I discovered, was evidence that the Spirit was already moving and working in me. This gave me hope that prayer was not based on my level of skill or discipline, because the Spirit was already actively leading me to new depths that I could not reach on my own. Your desire to pray is this same Spirit stirring within you.

Several years ago, God began to "teach me to pray" through the practice of imaginative prayer. My exploration came about slowly and intermittently, usually in groups with other Christians. We would be encouraged to imagine ourselves in a story from one of the Gospels as a way to interact with God in a more personal way. "Imagine you are on the boat with Jesus," a small group leader might say. Or "imagine you are standing at the foot of the cross." I always found these experiences meaningful and powerful as they ushered me into a new way of listening and watching Jesus in prayer. Though few and far between, these were my beginning forays into imaginative prayer.

Imaginative prayer invites us to focus our attention in prayer on Jesus and to open our eyes and ears to what he is doing and saying to us through the stories of his life in the Gospels. Imaginative prayer puts our feet into the sandals of those first disciples and asks Jesus to teach us to pray!

"IS THERE ANYBODY OUT THERE?"

This haunting song title from the 1979 Pink Floyd album, *The Wall*, gives voice to a deep question that many people, including Christians, feel from time to time. The movie, *The Wall*, is based on the music from the album and one scene shows Pink, the lead character, bashing up against a tremendously high wall desperately trying to listen through it or knock it over. The song plays eerily around him. As Christians, we might respond to this disturbing image by saying, "Of course someone is out there! *God.*" But when we allow ourselves the space to be honest we may discover this question lurking not far beneath the surface of our hearts. *Is* there anybody out there? *Is* God out there? Can God hear me? Can I hear God?

We might be afraid to ask these questions because we suspect that the answer is a crushing "No." Perhaps we *are* all alone. I have heard many people say that praying feels like talking to empty air or throwing words up to the ceiling only to have them crash in tatters at their feet. Because of this fear many of us will not risk being silent in prayer. We fill our prayers with lots of words, lots of noise and activity—our voices, our questions, even our praises—and then we quickly sign off so we do not have to face the deafening silence. We wonder if anyone is actually there who will respond to us. *Is there anybody out there?*

We ask this question longing for a response. We want to know that someone *is* there, listening to us and interacting with us. This is the core of prayer—real connection and relationship with God. Prayer is the primary place where we engage this relationship, where we deal with God, and turn our deepest selves toward God and communicate "face to face."[2] Eugene Peterson paints the following picture of prayer for us in his rendering of 2 Corinthians 3:16–18 (The Message):

> Whenever, though, they turn to face God as Moses did, God removes the veil and there they are—face to face! They suddenly recognize that God is a living personal presence, not a piece of chiseled stone . . . Nothing between us and God, our faces shining with the brightness of his face.

The words, "a living personal presence," powerfully stir our desire to pray. Is this not what we long for?

The prayer that seeks to know and experience this living personal presence of God face to face is often referred to as contemplative prayer. Contemplative prayer goes back at least as far as the monastic movements of the fourth and fifth centuries, if not the earliest recorded accounts of Scripture. Many of the psalms might be considered forms of contemplative prayer, as the psalmist is seeking God's face, listening to God, and responding to God. One simple way to think about contemplative prayer is that it is prayed from a posture of *receptivity*. We often think of prayer as something that *we* do. We ask, we seek, we confess, we praise. The word "prayer," typically, evokes an action on our part. Contemplative prayer, by contrast,

2. This metaphor comes from Exodus 33:11: "The LORD would speak to Moses face to face, as one speaks to a friend."

happens *to* us. As we open ourselves to receive the action and presence of God we move from focusing on ourselves to focusing on God. In contemplative prayer we are listening and watching for God.

While contemplative prayer is inviting, it is also risky because we find we are not in control. We must trust that there *is* "Someone out there" who will engage with us. When we cry out, "Is there anybody out there?" we do so with trepidation because we do not know if anyone will answer us. When we cry out with hope, faith, and longing, we take a real risk by supposing that there is a real Someone who is interested in communicating with us. We also may wonder what we will hear if there is a response? Will we be welcomed or condemned? Will we be loved or chastised? Whatever our theology might tell us about who God is, the invitation to engage is risky business. We take a risk every time we say, "Dear Lord."

Contemplative prayer is also difficult because we place ourselves in a position of immense vulnerability. If we are honest, we often approach prayer in order to get something out of it. We want to feel something, to receive an answer to our pressing question, or be comforted in our pain. We come with an agenda, and if our agenda is not met, we are frustrated. It is difficult to come with an openness to God and to lay aside our personal agenda. This requires a posture of waiting. And waiting is difficult. We find ourselves extremely vulnerable when we wait with expectation. Our culture does not train us to wait or to remain open and vulnerable. We want to take control and manage things but contemplative prayer demands waiting. We must wait in order to receive. It is tremendously difficult to resist our all-too-common tendencies to manipulate and dictate situations to our advantage and simply wait for God.

THE CONTEMPLATIVE POSTURE: RECEPTIVITY AND ATTENTIVENESS

Two stories in the Old Testament illustrate the contemplative stance of receptivity and attentiveness particularly well. In 1 Samuel 3, the young boy Samuel is living in the temple with Eli, the priest. One night as he is lying in his bed, he hears a voice calling to him, saying, "Samuel, Samuel."

Samuel gets up and goes to Eli.

"Here I am, master."

Eli asks what the boy wants.

"I heard you calling to me," says Samuel.

"I did not call you, son. Go back to bed," replies Eli. Samuel goes back to his bed, slightly confused. Perhaps he was dreaming. A few minutes go by.

Then again, he hears the voice saying, "Samuel, Samuel." Samuel dutifully gets up and heads back into Eli's room.

"Here I am, master."

Again, Eli sends him back to bed. He had not called the boy. Perhaps Eli is now wondering what the boy is up to.

Then a third time, Samuel hears the voice and presents himself to Eli.

"Ah," Eli sighs knowingly, "I know what's happening. It is the Lord calling you, son. The next time you hear the voice," he instructs the boy, "simply say, 'Speak Lord. I am listening.'" And so, when Samuel hears the voice again, he listens and responds.

Eli has taught Samuel an important lesson about prayer. "When the Lord speaks, be silent and listen." How often do we take time to listen in our prayer? Most, if not all, our prayers are filled with our own voice, our own thoughts, telling God all the details that are on our heart and mind. Aren't our prayers filled with our own words? Though we tend to think of prayer as our words to God, prayer includes God's word to us and so we need to include listening in our prayer. But listening is risky. Will God speak? Will we hear anything? How will we know?

The boy Samuel took a risk with his stance of waiting and listening. If we know this story, we know that God does speak to the boy, but can you imagine being this young boy at that moment, waiting on that night, in the dark? He has already heard the Voice calling him. Will he hear it again? Will the Voice say anything other than his name? What might the Voice demand of him? When we place ourselves into a story like this, all these questions become our questions, questions that may be deep within us but have yet to find their voice.

A second story. In 2 Kings 6, Elisha, the prophet, has raised the ire of the Aramean army by giving away all their military secrets to the Israelite army. Understandably, the Arameans are not happy, and so they make plans to kill Elisha. They find out where he lives and march down upon his little house. Elisha's servant boy, Gehazi, who is perhaps out in the yard doing some tasks, sees the massive army descending upon them. He is terrified and runs to Elisha.

"Master, Master! The army. We're done for!"

Elisha seems oddly unconcerned. I imagine him walking out the door, slowly drying off his hands with a towel after washing up and looking across the valley to the army as it bears down upon them. He looks at the boy, then at the army, then at the boy again. A small smile emerges on his face. Gehazi is dumbstruck. Does he not see the army? Is the old man crazy?

Calmly, Elisha begins to pray. I imagine him putting his hand gently on the boy's head.

"Open his eyes, Lord, so he might see." Immediately, the eyes of the boy are opened, and he sees the vast army of the Lord, replete with angels and chariots, completely surrounding the enemy.

Elisha, like Eli before him, instructs the boy, and us, how to pray. "Open your eyes. The Lord wants to show you something. Look. Watch." Can you imagine this young boy's experience? As he looks out over the imposing army, his heart pounds in fear, but then suddenly—or, perhaps, slowly, and almost imperceptibly—he begins to see another army beyond. As he continues to look into the distance the landscape changes. His gaze rises above and beyond the army directly in front of him. Are those chariots? Soldiers? Angels?

My prayers usually consist of the things that I can see and feel directly, the realities of my life that I see right in front of me. My prayers are mostly filled with my immediate needs, my family, my friends, my thoughts, my ideas. Here, listening to Elisha, I learn to take a different stance in prayer. I learn to ask for sight to see a deeper reality, a fuller and more *real* reality. I learn to wait and watch for what might emerge above and beyond my usual sightlines. Mostly, I learn to ask to be healed of my blindness. *Open my eyes, Lord.*

While these incidents in the lives of these biblical characters may not seem to be specifically about prayer, they *are* stories about humans interacting with God and as such they can teach us about the *relational* nature of prayer as a way of communicating with God. We tend to limit prayer to the particular action of sitting and thinking silent thoughts or voicing pious words but prayer engages our whole lives and imaginative prayer can help us experience prayer in a more holistic way.

The essence of contemplative and imaginative prayer is conveyed in Samuel's stance of receptive waiting and listening and Gehazi's attentive watching. Rather than doing all the talking ourselves, this form of prayer invites us to look beyond our usual horizons. "*Lord, open our eyes to see and our ears to hear you.*"

By praying with our imagination we can practice this contemplative posture of receptivity and attentiveness. As we wait, listen, and watch Jesus within the context of the Gospel stories we are invited to enter into these stories, imagining that we are actually in the scene, watching and listening for what is happening around us. The stories are not about us, per se, and so we can simply watch and wait for Jesus to act. We enter the story as guests, anticipating how the Lord might be calling us to listen or see anew.

HOW DID JESUS PRAY?

Jesus himself must have prayed in a contemplative fashion, using his imagination. We are told a few times in the Gospels that Jesus "went out to a mountainside to pray" (Luke 6:12) or "very early in the morning, while it was still dark, Jesus got up, left the house and went off to a solitary place, where he prayed" (Mark 1:35). Except for only a few times we are not told what these prayers were like. What did Jesus' experience in these times of prayer? What did he say? What did he hear? John 17 offers the longest recorded prayer of Jesus in the Bible. In that prayer, Jesus prays for himself, for his friends, and for all who will come after him. Based on this prayer and Jesus' instructions to his disciples about how to pray in Matthew 6 ("The Lord's Prayer"), you might be left with the impression that prayer consists in speaking to God, petitioning God, and worshiping God. This is how most of us have learned to pray and so we use words to ask God for what we need and to express our praise, gratitude, and worship. This is a fundamentally biblical way to pray.

But the Gospels also teach us indirectly about another reality in Jesus' prayer life. When Jesus is confronted by the unbelieving Pharisees who refused to trust him, he says that none of his words come from himself alone. "The Father who sent me gave me orders, told me *what to say* and *how to say it* . . . What the Father told me, I tell you" (John 12:49–50, The Message, emphasis added). How did Jesus know what the Father wanted him to say? And how did he know the manner in which the Father wanted him to say it? Somehow, Jesus had heard the Father. He was listening.

Earlier in John 5, Jesus tells the unbelieving religious leaders, "Very truly I tell you, the Son can do nothing by himself; he can only do what he *sees* his Father doing" (v. 19, emphasis added). How could he see what the Father was doing? How could he see beyond his natural human eyesight? Jesus could perceive what his father was doing because his eyes were open, and he was *watching* for a reality that was not readily perceptible to everyone else. He was able to see the way Elisha—and eventually Gehazi—could see. Listening and watching is a significant part of the relational dynamic between Jesus and his father.

We do not know precisely what this looked like for Jesus, how or what he heard or how or what he saw. But we can enter this way of praying by using the gift of our imaginations and intentionally watching and listening inside the context of the Gospel stories. We can *practice* watching and listening the way Jesus watched and listened to his father. We are not left on our own to figure out some technique Jesus used to perceive his father's movements. Through the gift of the Spirit, we have been given this ability to *see* and *hear* what is not readily perceptible to human eyes and ears. As we practice this gift and cultivate our relationship with Jesus we will take on his eyes and ears and learn to trust him and love him just as he trusted and loved his father.

DISCOVERING JESUS

If you were raised as I was, in the Evangelical tradition, you have likely heard the invitation to "invite Jesus into your heart." This is a shorthand way to talk about conversion. Many people will be able to name the day, even the time, that they "made a decision for Christ." Memories like this can act as a bulwark against future doubts and questions, when the realities of life's suffering, and pain, along with our own disappointments and failures, cause us to question God's presence with us and within us. We name these conversion experiences as "inviting Jesus into our heart."[3] Such decisions invite Jesus to have access to our true selves so that we can enter into a place of intimacy and relationship with him. When we invite Jesus into our life and heart we are saying that we care deeply about him and desire to follow him and live our life for him.

However, we are also invited to make an even more fundamental decision, to accept God's invitation to enter into *his* life. When I invite Jesus into my life I can remain the primary subject, the main person in the

---

3. Many Christians cannot name the time or day when they made such a decision. Those who grow up in Christian families may have a much more gradual experience of coming to faith. We will see this dynamic playing out as we reflect on the "stages" of friendship where the movement from one stage to another might be quite sudden and dramatic or rather gradual and only noticeable in hindsight.

relationship. I can be asking Jesus to come along with me, to help me, guide me, and love me. This is all well and good when we first begin to follow Jesus because we are not quite sure we can fully trust him at the beginning of our relationship and so we invite him to come along with us as we continue to live our lives hoping that he will be involved and helpful.

But as we listen to Jesus, as the relationship turns more and more into an intimate friendship, he starts saying things like, "You must lay down your life, you must give away everything, you must follow me." This is something else entirely. Jesus will not allow us to continue thinking that he has hitched a ride onto our life. Being a friend of Jesus is far more costly. He plans to change us. He starts asking us to turn away from the life we thought we needed, away from the life we are so busily and frantically creating, to leave everything and follow him. C.S. Lewis asks us to imagine our life as a house that needs renovations. When we invite Jesus to live in our house, he begins his renovation project by fixing the drains and stopping up the leaky roof. We like this. We need these repairs. But soon enough:

> He starts knocking the house about in a way that hurts abominably and does not seem to make any sense. What on earth is He up to? The explanation is that He is building quite a different house from the one you thought of—throwing out a new wing here, putting on an extra floor there, running up towers, making courtyards. You thought you were being made into a decent little cottage: but He is building a palace. He intends to come and live in it Himself.[4]

God is building a new house altogether, a new life in us. We do not see Jesus joining Peter and Andrew in their fishing business, bringing them success and a good life. We do not see Jesus joining Matthew in his tax collecting enterprise, or Simon in his zealotry. Jesus asks everyone—his disciples, his friends, you, me—to lay down our lives and follow him, into the unknown. This is the process of friend-making that Jesus embarks on with us when we say "Yes" to him. Initially, we may fear this will result in our dissolution because we cannot imagine a life that we have not constructed ourselves and so we hang on desperately to our old life. But a new house is already under construction by the master carpenter and he asks us to join in the work he is doing and to lay our plans to the side. He does this by inviting us into friendship. Mysteriously, we discover our lives are not diminished in this process. Being a friend of Jesus opens us up to where our true life is to be found.

4. Lewis, *Mere Christianity*, 174.

When we come to pray imaginatively with the stories in the Gospels we are invited to enter *into* the Jesus story, to focus on him, listen to him and watch him as he lives his life. These stories are not from our lives; they are from Jesus' life, and we are invited into *them*. As we do this more and more we will discover that a friendship is developing and we find within us the courage and the gift to actually follow Jesus the way we deeply want to.

LIVING WITH JESUS

Many of us have grown up with the stories from the Gospels, and we may think we have already learned what we are supposed to learn from them. Even those of us who have come to these stories later in life may approach them as tools to teach us about God, life, and living in the kingdom of God. We often approach the whole Bible as a book that teaches us about God, Jesus, and the Spirit—which of course, it does. But the fundamental purpose of the biblical narrative is not to be simply a teaching tool. No real stories should be exploited in this way. All stories, by their nature, invite us to participate, to bring our whole selves, emotions, thoughts, and actions into the story and allow it to work its way into our hearts and imaginations. When we fully engage in stories, we are changed. How much more, then, will we be changed by Gospel stories which unveil for us the life of Jesus, the author and perfecter of our faith? The stories in the Gospels convey the grand story of God as it was lived through Jesus' life and they invite us to enter into them prayerfully, through our imaginations, so that we can live these stories into our own lives.

While we learn many things about people, relationships, and life from our experiences each day, *learning* is not our primary stance toward living. We do not meet up with a friend to *learn* something from them. Rather, we want to experience the gift of their friendship. Because we care about them, we want to share our life with them. While we may end up learning something in a derivative way, the fundamental goal is the simple experience of being *with* them. Our *relationship* is more essential than knowledge. (In Ephesians 3:19, Paul says something like this when he prays that the early Jesus followers will experience Christ's love, "that surpasses knowledge").

As Christians, we study the Bible, listen to sermons, and read books to learn more about our faith, but prayer offers us a unique opportunity to encounter Jesus as a friend. We enter into prayer as a way to connect with

God, listen to him, receive from him, express our hearts to him, and live more closely with him.

This book invites you to enter into the Gospels through imaginative prayer in order to meet, love, and live with Jesus. This way of praying beckons you to engage with Jesus in relational and personal ways as you watch him interact with others and experience his interactions with you. This is how friendships are formed. Whenever we practice imaginative prayer, we return again and again to what Eugene Peterson describes as the "living personal presence" of God.

LISTENING TO THE WORD OF LOVE

Ignatius Loyola, the founder of the Jesuits in the sixteenth century, encouraged those who were preparing to engage his *Spiritual Exercises* to take some time and establish a solid foundation of God's love before they embarked on the prayer journey proper. Before entering into Jesus' life as it is depicted in the Gospels, we will take some time and space to allow God's love to become firmly established within us. It is easy to make the mistake of rushing into prayer, especially if we have been Christians for a long time. We may think we already know how to pray, but Paul tells us there are times when, "we do not know what we ought to pray for" (Romans 8:26). We are wise to listen to this, coming humbly to the Lord, listening for his words of love and care for us.

The following imaginative prayer exercises will help us prepare for the journey ahead by focusing our attention on God's abiding love for us so that when we encounter Jesus in the Gospels we will already know deep within our heart, mind, body, and soul that we are fully seen, known, and loved. The emphasis in these exercises is on listening to and receiving these words of God, taking the posture of young Samuel, "Speak, Lord, I am listening."

IMAGINATIVE PRAYER EXERCISE: BECOMING ROOTED IN GOD'S LOVE (PSALM 139:1-13)

Find a place of quiet where you will be undisturbed for several minutes; a place where you can relax and listen well in an unhurried way. Now imagine Jesus sitting beside you. After you sit together in silence for a minute or two, imagine Jesus begins to speak the words of Psalm 139 over you:

I have searched you, (your name) and I know you,[5]
I know when you sit and when you rise.
I perceive your thoughts from afar
I discern your going out and your lying down,
I am familiar with all your ways . . .
If you say, 'Surely the darkness will hide me
and the light become night around me,"
Even the darkness will not be dark to me;
the night will shine like the day
for darkness is as light to me . . .
I created your inmost being, [your name]
I knit you together in your mother's womb."

After a brief pause, imagine Jesus repeating these words again. As they flow over you, listen to them carefully and imagine Jesus speaking them directly to you. Then imagine Jesus repeating these words a third time. As you hear them again, picture them as a solid foundation being formed beneath you, establishing the reality of God's care and love for you. These words are solid. These words are truth. Now, sit in that reality and ask the Spirit to send these words deep into your bones. Listen to the truth of God's love for you over and over. Linger with these words and let them water the soil of your mind and heart. Open your hands and imagine yourself receiving the gift of these words, the gift of Jesus' loving presence.

IMAGINATIVE PRAYER EXERCISE: TRUSTING IN THE REALITY OF GOD'S LOVE (ISAIAH 43:1-7)

This passage from Isaiah can prepare us for our prayer journey by grounding us in the truth that God chooses us and loves us beyond measure. Imagine yourself taking a walk with Jesus through a familiar place where you enjoy spending time. After a minute of two, Jesus stops, turns toward you, and begins speaking the following words:

Do not fear, [your name], *for I have redeemed you:*
I have summoned you by name, you are mine.
When you pass through the waters, I will be with you;
and when you pass through the rivers, they will not sweep over you.
When you walk through the fire, you will not be burned:
the flames will not set you ablaze. (vv.1–3)

5. I have taken the liberty to change this psalm into the first person, as if the Lord is speaking this directly to you.

God spoke these words to the people of Israel to remind them of God's promise to be with them and to protect them. By following Jesus, you have been incorporated into this story. Israel's story is now your story.

The prayer continues. Jesus looks directly at you and says, "[Your name], *you are precious and honored in my sight . . . and I love you*" (v. 4). As you hear these words, you sense God inviting you to listen to the truth that you are "precious" in his sight, that he "honors" you and loves you, that he is willing to do whatever it takes to find you and bring you home. Linger here for awhile. Do not rush off. Allow these words to permeate deeply to your core.

CHAPTER 2

Engaging Our Imagination in Prayer

I know of no better argument for placing imagination
at the heart of God's dealings with us
than the single, unique, unpredicted, and unpredictable
event of the Incarnation.[1]

—John McIntyre

Taste and see that the Lord is good;
blessed is the one who takes refuge in him.

—Psalm 34:8

BEFORE TIM AND I set out on our trip, we had to decide how we were going to travel. We landed on cycling. We thought this would be a great way to see the country but we knew that we needed particular bikes that could withstand the unknown territory we might be traveling in Australia. We were not planning anything extreme but we did not know what we might find once we got there—neither of us had been to Australia before. Mountain bikes were fairly new then and they seemed the perfect fit for our adventure. We had both been riding bikes since we were kids but because of the extent of our trip and the newness of these bikes, we took some time to familiarize ourselves with all the features that were part of these mountain bikes.

1. McIntyre, *Faith, Theology, and Imagination*, 55.

They were equipped with fifteen gears, a rear harness for our backpacks and water, and knobby tires for any kind of terrain. They were perfect.

Our prayer journey requires its own piece of "equipment"—our imagination. The good news is that it is already packed for us. Though we may feel that our imagination is dull, misplaced, or impoverished, we use it all the time whether we know it or not. When we think about something—an elephant, a cat, our closest friend—our imagination is activated as we picture these things in our mind. We were all created with this ability to imagine things in our minds that we cannot see with our eyes. This amazing ability is so integral to the way our minds work that we tend not to think of it as anything extraordinary.

The work of our imagination is so deeply ingrained in us that it continues even as we sleep. We *see* things in our minds that are not actually present—and it often feels very real! Many of us have had dreams that are so vivid that our bodies respond as if we are actually experiencing them—we start to sweat, our heart rate increases, we toss around in our beds, perhaps we cry out or speak. When we wake up it can feel as if we were actually involved in the activity of our dream.

Neuroscience researchers have studied the link between physical action (what is seen) and imagined action (what is unseen) and discovered a powerful connection between the imagination and the body. In *The Brain that Changes Itself*, Norman Doidge describes a series of experiments by noted researcher Alvaro Pascual-Leone of Harvard Medical School.[2] Pascual-Leone took two groups of people and taught them a simple sequence of notes on the piano. None of the participants in either group had ever studied the piano. One group practiced for two hours each day for five days. The other group sat in front of a piano and *imagined* playing the notes and producing the sounds for two hours a day for five days. Doidge writes, "Both groups learned to play the sequence [of notes] . . . Remarkably, mental practice alone produced the same physical changes in the motor system as actually playing the piece . . . The imagining players were as accurate as the actual players."[3] The imagined activity of the mind had produced a profound effect on the body. This has significant implications for our spiritual lives.

2. Doidge, *Brain that Changes Itself*, 201.
3. Doidge, *Brain that Changes Itself*, 201.

PRAYING WITH THE IMAGINATION

When we pray with our imagination, watching Jesus and imagining him in our minds, our bodies can begin to incorporate his actions as we live our day-to-day lives. Author and philosopher James K.A. Smith describes the process as follows:

> To conform to the image of the Son is to have so absorbed the gospel as a "kinesthetic sense," a know-how you now carry in your bones, that you do by "feel" what cannot be done by conscious thought . . . You have a Christlike "feel" for the world, and you act accordingly "without even thinking about it." This kind of "sense" is deeper than knowledge: it's a know-how you absorb poetically, on the register of the imagination.[4]

Watching Jesus in imaginative prayer is a way to *absorb* his way of living, his way of being into our bodies. Like the Harvard research participants who imagined themselves as piano players, our imaginations can help us live more like Jesus in the world.

The imagination also holds emotional content. For example, when we take someone's hand, our brain fires off dozens of neurons that connect the experience of touch with the emotions that accompany that activity. We not only feel the other's physical hand, we also experience the warmth and affection of holding hands. When we *imagine* taking someone's hand, many of these same neurons are activated. Can you remember the first time you held hands with your teenage crush? Your memory, through your imagination, *holds* that powerful feeling. Even when we are no longer physically touching that person's hand, we can experience the warmth, affection, and emotional connection in our minds.

For the same reason, traumatic experiences continue to have negative effects on us long after the initial trauma. We may remember and continue to feel the pain of the original experience and we may find ourselves reliving the trauma over and over again in our minds—to the point where we can become debilitated. Though the experience may have been far in the past, the emotions generated by our imagination are especially present to us and very real. Our bodies will continue to react to these inner sensations. We may tense up, or begin to weep, or react strongly to someone's touch. The imagination is a powerful conduit of emotions and memories.

---

4. Smith, *You Are What You Love*, 108.

Interestingly, Jesus spoke to this connection between the mind and body through the imagination. When he tells his disciples in the Sermon on the Mount (Matthew 5:28) that lustfully looking at a woman (or a man) is essentially the same as committing adultery with them in the body, he is affirming the power of the imagination to activate our minds, emotions, wills, and thoughts. He makes no distinction between the physical act and the imagined act on our consciences. The imagination has an immense power to shape and form us in destructive ways, often leading to physical and emotional pain for us and others—yet all of it happens in our minds!

This raises a question about how we might actively form our imagination rather than being passive recipients of its influence. How can we point our imagination toward God, allowing him to shape it rather than it shaping us in ways we do not want? Northrup Frye, the late literary critic, says:

> We use our imaginations all the time: it comes into all our conversation and practical life, it even produces dreams when we sleep. Consequently, we only have the choice between a badly trained imagination and a well-trained one.[5]

What might it look like to *train* our imagination? Frye would likely contend for reading great literature and allowing it to form our imaginations toward the good, the true, and the beautiful. This is excellent advice but does not go far enough. Our imaginations, as with our entire lives, have been created to bring glory to God by drawing us into deeper union with Christ. Praying with our imagination, intentionally bringing our imaginative abilities into our prayer with Jesus, is one way that our imagination can be healed, nurtured, and transformed. As we pray with our imagination, we partner with God's activity of renewing and redeeming every aspect of our being—and, indeed, the whole world.

For many years, I volunteered with a discipleship ministry that helped people walk away from destructive patterns of sexual fantasy and addictions. The imaginations of those who were seeking help from this ministry had been seared and distorted because they had used their imagination to self-medicate and embrace lust and fantasy, seeking fulfillment and satisfaction apart from God. When we activate the imagination this way we become trapped and enslaved to fantasies and patterns of thinking that can seem impossible to break. When we are caught in this kind of cyclical trap the imagination seems to be the problem rather than a tool for healing.

5. Frye, "Abandoning Earth," para 4.

Instead of trying to ignore these unholy fantasies and thought patterns or trying hard to think and act differently, those who feel enslaved to their thoughts can invite Jesus *into* these sinful patterns and allow him to bring his healing presence. My own healing in this area came from recognizing that Jesus was present with me right in the middle of my sin and shame, loving me and calling me out of my sin rather than being disappointed and disgusted with me. Imagining Jesus being with me *in the flesh* was far more powerful than merely *thinking* about his love conceptually. When I thought of an abstract Jesus that "loved" me, my shame and guilt would quickly overwhelm and dismiss his love, but when I imagined Jesus standing next to me and embracing me, his love became physical and I found myself wanting to follow him out of my sinful patterns. His presence with me was powerful! Love now had a face.

When we turn our imagination toward Jesus rather than using it to turn away from him, our mind begins to heal and transformation can occur. Our imagination gives us this ability to turn toward Jesus by entering into his life as it is portrayed in the Gospels. We can imagine his physical presence, his voice, his eyes, his touch. By praying in this way, we are able to practice Paul's admonition in Philippians 4:8 in regard to Jesus himself: "Whatever is true, whatever is noble, whatever is right, whatever is pure, whatever is lovely, whatever is admirable—if anything is excellent or praiseworthy—think about such things." Our imagination is a gift that enables us to embrace the presence and reality of Jesus.

THE LANGUAGE OF THE IMAGINATION

The Scriptures, interestingly, are full of the language of the imagination—symbols, metaphors, and narratives. Having the freedom to communicate in any way at all, God has seen fit to use imaginative communication to reveal Godself to us in Scripture. In *Between the Image and the Word*, Trevor Hart describes this rich language.

> The same Old Testament which . . . urged the abandonment of *material* representations of God, elsewhere encourages and fuels an abundant and diverse poetic 'imaging' of him on more or less every page (as king, shepherd, warrior, rock, lion, strength and shield, light and so on).[6]

---

6. Hart, *Between the Image and the Word*, 39.

As we read Scripture, the metaphorical imagery invites us to engage our imagination as a way to seek and find God.

The poetic and imaginative revelation of God is particularly apparent in the book of Psalms. In Psalm 1, the "blessed" person is like "a tree planted by steams of water which yields its fruit in season" (v. 3). In Psalm 23, God is imaged as the good shepherd, and we are imaged as God's sheep. In Psalm 36, we read that God's love "reaches to the heavens . . . your righteousness is like the highest mountains" (v.:5–6). As the ancient prayer book of the people of God, the book of Psalms connects prayer with the imagination constantly, using images, symbols, and metaphors to describe God and his relationship with his people. These metaphors and images draw us energetically into the action as participants. These are not simply words to be admired. They are hands that grab us and invite us to dance. Eugene Peterson describes the power of metaphor this way:

> A metaphor is a compressed story and as a metaphor embeds itself in our consciousness it begins to tell a story that involves us. It is hard to maintain passivity in the presence of a metaphor. Metaphor makes it difficult to continue as a bystander, coolly watching the action. Metaphor pulls us into an involved participation in what the writer or speaker of the metaphor is about.[7]

Metaphors and stories create images in our minds that pull us into a scene or situation with our whole selves—our minds, our bodies, and our lives.

As James K.A. Smith notes, the Bible *might* have come to us as a series of rational, ordered, and logical teachings, but it did not.

> If the biblical narrative of God's redemption were just information we needed to know, the Lord could have simply given us a book and a whole lot of homework . . . the gospel isn't just information stored in the intellect; it is a way of seeing the world that is the very wallpaper of our imagination.[8]

Instead of presenting us with a textbook, the Bible offers us a diverse conglomerate of stories, metaphors, symbols, and parables that all require us to engage our imagination. To know God, Scripture seems to be saying, one must utilize the imagination.

Our modern era has set aside the imagination in favor of more rationalistic approaches to spiritual knowledge and practice. Many people think

---

7. Peterson, *Jesus Way,* 215.
8. Smith, *You Are What You Love,* 107.

that being imaginative means making up *imaginary* things and assume that the imagination is only for those who want a creative outlet. *Real* knowledge, our culture asserts, is scientific knowledge that can be tested and verified scientifically. Kathleen Fischer writes, "We associate imagination with emotion and intuition, and we in the West have been schooled to regard these as sources of error and deception."[9] We use phrases like "It's just your imagination" to fuel the sense that the imagination only reveals fantasy or irrational fears. If we think this way about the imagination, then it will not have a place in our spiritual life. But if we look at the way Jesus taught his disciples, we can see that the imagination is essential for understanding and living the spiritual life.

JESUS THE STORYTELLER

Have you ever heard a gifted storyteller weave a tale, drawing you in, surprising you, and delighting you? Eugene Peterson was fond of recounting how he would sit with his grandchildren after telling them a story, and one of them would inevitably cry out, "Grandpa, tell us another story, and make sure we're in it!"[10] Good stories invite us in. We want to find ourselves living inside them.

Stories are the lifeblood of our imagination. When a story begins our imagination is awakened and immediately begins making connections and evoking emotions. As we are drawn in, we hope that we will discover something new or captivating, something that will give shape to our own storied lives. Jesus understands our human love for stories. Throughout his teaching ministry he uses stories, metaphors, and other tools of the imagination to enthrall his listeners and draw them in. He tells stories to help people imagine a different way of thinking, living, and being. He tells stories about his father and the kingdom of God in order to paint a picture of a new kind of life. He wants people to be able to *see* and *taste* this new life—and so he engages his listeners' imaginations.

The parables of Jesus act as fuel on the embers of our imagination. Stories envelop us, connect with our hearts, and move us emotionally. After listening to a compelling story, we respond from a deep place within ourselves because our minds, emotions, and wills have been stirred. Jesus could have used facts, arguments, and propositional statements to teach

9. Fischer, *Inner Rainbow*, 6.

10. I heard Peterson say this in a course on prayer at Regent College in the early 1990s.

people about God but he chooses to use stories. If we believe that the *content* of Scripture is inspired by God, we must also recognize that the *form* is also inspired.

Many people in the Gospels respond emotionally to the stories of Jesus because they discover themselves *in* the story. It is as if these stories are actually happening to *them*. Jesus knows that stories will draw in his listeners and evoke a heart response. He does not seem interested in simply relaying information so he uses the imagination to capture people at a much deeper level.

When we use our imagination in prayer we follow in the footsteps of Jesus. Just as Jesus tells stories to draw in his listeners, the Gospel writers do the same, presenting stories that invite us to experience the reality of Jesus through our imagination. Throughout the Gospels, we see those who spend time with Jesus interacting with him as they would with anyone—speaking to him, listening to him, observing him, enjoying him, just as we all do with people in our lives. Imaginative prayer helps us imagine interacting with Jesus in the flesh like his first followers did. Imagining a scene and allowing it to impact us is different than listening to an essay about abstract concepts like love and forgiveness. When we pray imaginatively we move beyond a conceptual understanding of Jesus toward an actual encounter with him, in ways very similar to our experience of any relationship in our lives.

We are embodied spiritual beings with immense imaginative capabilities. Our minds connect the seen with the unseen, link our internal images with our physical bodies, and carry the emotional weight of memories and experience. The Bible itself weaves together an imaginative matrix of narrative, story and metaphor that invites us to engage our imaginations as we seek the face of the One in whose image we are made.

In the next chapter, we will discuss how to engage our imaginations in prayer in more detail, but first let us practice entering into a story from the Gospels using your imagination.

AN IMAGINATIVE PRAYER EXERCISE: THE WIDOW OF NAIN (LUKE 7:11–17)

Read through this story about the widow of Nain in Luke's Gospel. Because we have all seen so many "impossible" things happen in movies and television, we can probably imagine the scene of the son coming back from the dead, but it most likely has little emotional impact on us. But the Gospel says the people who witnessed this event were "filled with awe" (NIV). The NRSVA renders it even more powerfully; "Fear seized all of them." The Greek word used here is the same word used in the story of the disciples witnessing Jesus walking on the water thinking it was a ghost (Matthew 14:26). These people could not believe their eyes, and so they look at Jesus and exclaim, "A great prophet has appeared among us!" This is the kind of experience that we desire as we enter into these stories. We want it to feel real, to feel what we would actually feel if it happened in our real life. Sometimes, we may want to put the scene into our modern reality as a way to get closer to the action and experience. We will do this with the following story, putting it in a modern-day context rather than in the first century.

Imagine yourself at the funeral of a family member or friend. Once you have placed yourself at that funeral, allow the story to unfold.

~

The funeral service is nearly finished. You look across at all the family members and friends who have gathered to remember this person whom you all loved. Who is it that has died? What memories surface about this beloved person in your life?

Your eyes move to the coffin at the front of the church. What emotions are stirring up for you? Sit with these feelings and memories for a few minutes.

You watch the pallbearers come to the front, lift the coffin off the table, and walk slowly down the aisle. As they pass by, look directly at their faces. What do you see?

As the family walks down the aisle you fall in behind the procession.

In the foyer, people are murmuring and embracing each other. Then a man you don't recognize stops the pallbearers and speaks to them. The man turns to a family member and says, "Don't cry," but before anyone can respond the man touches the coffin and says, "I say, get up!"

What goes through your mind when the man says this? How does everyone around you respond?

Suddenly, you see the lid of the coffin rising, and then your loved one sits up and starts talking! What do they say? How do you respond? How do others respond? What do you feel?

Then you look at the man who told your loved one to get up and you realize he is Jesus.

What do you want to say to him? What emotions are you feeling?

After reflecting on this scene for several minutes, allow it to slowly fade.

CHAPTER 3

The Practice Run

Prayer cannot be measured on a scale of success and failure
because it is God's work and God always succeeds.[1]

—Michael Casey

Let us draw near to God with a sincere heart and with the
full assurance that faith brings.

—Hebrews 10:22

WHEN TIM AND I purchased our bikes for our trip, they were still in their original boxes. We got them home and eagerly opened them, assembling and disassembling them several times—we were going to have to do this many times for plane travel—and took them out on the street for a test ride. We knew how to ride bikes, obviously, but we wanted to see how these particular bikes would handle in various terrains and weather conditions. We wanted to know they were in good working order before we set out on our journey. One of the mistakes we made was neglecting to train and get our *bodies* in good working order. Halfway through the first day we were writhing around on the ground, our legs screaming, unable to get in a comfortable position to stop the pain of our out-of-shape leg muscles. The only thing we could do was to keep going.

1. Casey, *Toward God*, 35.

Before venturing out on our prayer journey we want to "test drive" the equipment we will be using—our imagination—so that we have a good sense of how to engage with the stories as we come to them. Any "training" that we may need will happen along the way on the journey. Like any new form of prayer, we simply bring our desires and our time, trusting that the Lord will meet us and lead us into new territory. While this chapter will make specific suggestions about how to engage our imagination in prayer, it is not outlining the *right* way to do this. Rather, it is sketching a rough map that can guide us as we set off on our prayer journey.

It is always dangerous to offer specific instruction about how to pray. It is far too easy to rely on certain techniques and methods as pathways to obtain what we desire through prayer. As Ann Ulanov warns us, all our methods of prayer are "mere gropings in the dark."[2] Nothing that we do can force a particular experience in prayer. Encounter with Jesus is always by grace, utterly and completely. He is the one who initiates toward us. All we are able to do is pay attention, to put ourselves in a posture of watching and listening for how God may be speaking to us, and then to respond to his love. We would do well to heed Michael Casey's word above, that our notions of "success" or "failure" in prayer are off the mark. We do not control. We simply submit.

Sleeping has a similar dynamic. We cannot *make* ourselves sleep. Sleep is a gift and comes on its own. Yet we are not completely passive. If we want to sleep, we do not keep walking around the house, eating, or doing exercise. If we want to sleep, we will put ourselves into a position to welcome sleep. We will lie down on a comfortable mattress. We will turn off the lights. We may even try to slow our breathing. All these actions prepare us for sleep but they do not guarantee it. Sleep must be given. In the same way we can position ourselves to pray. We can focus our mind. We can ask for grace. But we cannot force an encounter with Jesus. Jesus must come to us.[3]

This chapter offers some basic guidelines about how to prepare ourselves to engage our imagination in prayer. If this is new to you, keep in mind that the more we engage our imagination, the more it develops.

---

2. Ulanov, *Picturing God,* 93.
3. Smith, *Imagining the Kingdom,* 65.

MAPPING THE JOURNEY

When praying imaginatively, we are hoping to experience the Gospel story as it unfolds in real time so it is important to give ourselves several minutes of uninterrupted prayer. When we slow down our minds and allow the imagined scene to unfold, we need to give our hearts the time to listen and respond.

After setting aside a spacious window of time, ask the Spirit to give you the desire to pray. As Thomas Merton reminds us:

> Anyone who imagines he can simply begin meditating without praying for the desire and the grace to do so will soon give up. But the desire to meditate, and the grace to begin meditating, should be taken as an implicit promise of further graces.[4]

We need God's help to pray! We need the Spirit's presence and power as we seek the Lord's presence. We do not pray alone through our own power. Though we are praying *to* God, it is God's grace to us that fans into flame our desire to pray.

Once you have selected a Gospel story, (or come to the stories in this book), read it slowly and carefully two or three times. After the scene and the action of the story are firmly in your mind, read through the passage again, noticing any little details that will enhance the setting. Then close your eyes and imagine the scene, trying to place yourself *in* the scene. You might be standing on the side of the road while Jesus and his disciples pass by or sitting on the floor in a house where Jesus is teaching. Begin a few minutes before the action of the scene so that you can get situated and notice your surroundings. Pay attention to all that you see, hear, and smell. Is it busy or quiet? Who else is there? What landmarks or objects do you notice around you? Is it morning or evening? What details catch your eye? How are you feeling—fearful? Excited? Tired? Bored?

Once you are situated in the scene begin to imagine the action of the story, remaining present *as if* you are physically in the scene. Allow the scene to unfold slowly. We have been taught to read the Gospel stories as whole units, along with the "lessons" we are meant to learn from them. But this is not how we experience life. In life, one thing happens after another. Let your actions and emotions emerge naturally as you watch the scene unfold, responding to what you are experiencing, just like you do in life.

---

4. As cited in Foster, *Prayer*, 153.

Our desire is to *experience* the story rather than simply reading it. We usually interact with biblical stories by reading them as experiences other people had with Jesus. Yet through our imagination, we might think of these stories as real experiences that have been captured, like a photograph, in our spiritual memory. Old Testament theologian A.J. Culp describes this process, explaining how Scripture uses memory to help readers experience a historical narrative within their current reality. In Deuteronomy, Moses tells the people to "remember" the events of the Exodus even though many of them did not experience those events themselves. Similarly, at the Last Supper, Jesus tells his disciples (and all his followers) to "remember me," not in a nostalgic way but as a way to bring his imminent death into their (and our) present reality. The Eucharist brings this communal memory into our lived reality now. Thus we "remember" the stories of Jesus in the Gospels as "our" stories rather than merely reading them as stories about others. This act of remembering brings these stories closer to our own experience.[5]

Experiencing a story is different from *thinking* about it or *learning* something from it. Of course, we will learn from biblical stories but our longing in prayer is to enter into them in an experiential way. When we pray imaginatively with these stories we are hoping to encounter Jesus. When we observe an action or engage in a conversation with a friend we are not thinking about what we are supposed to learn from the experience. We simply notice what we are experiencing and feel the accompanying emotions. When we are *present* to a situation our emotions are much closer to the surface because we are not distancing ourselves by analyzing the situation. When we enter Gospel stories through imaginative prayer, we *live in them* and notice things we might not register when simply reading them. It may take some time to make this shift. If you find yourself wondering about what you should be learning from a story, gently lay that aside and pay attention to what is unfolding in front of you in the scene.

As you allow the story to unfold before you, take special notice of Jesus. How do you imagine his voice? What does he look like? What color are his eyes? How does he walk? How tall is he? Is he muscular? Thin? You might be surprised by the Jesus of your imagination! Of course, no one really knows what Jesus actually looked like,[6] but his unique facial features

5. Culp, "A.J. Culp—Memoirs of Moses," *OnScript* podcast.

6. One caveat: Jesus was a Middle Eastern Jew, not a North American Caucasian man. In our day of heightened awareness of our captivity to ethnic identities, recognizing that Jesus was not a "white man" might help us who are white to lay down our ethnic identity in order to follow him. See Taylor, "What Did Jesus Really Look Like?" for an interesting discussion of this.

and his voice had a distinctive cadence. If we find this exercise difficult, it could be that we are having a hard time accepting that Jesus was actually a full human being who desires to interact with us.

I once led this exercise with a group of pastors and one pastor claimed he did not have much of an imagination. He was a man of facts. He had been a farmer most of his life and had not entered pastoral work until his late fifties. He said he was used to swinging a hammer, not creating images in his mind, but he was willing to give it a try.

After the exercise, I could tell that this man was deep in thought. After several other people shared, he said that he had been unable to get into the story, and so he simply imagined himself sitting on the back deck of his house. He was waiting for the exercise to end when he noticed Jesus walking around the corner of his house. "But he was wearing coveralls and a plaid shirt!" the pastor said with a huge grin. "I couldn't believe that Jesus would show up like that! I figured he would be in robes and all glowing or something, but he was wearing the same clothes I love to wear." Tears welled up in his eyes as he quietly finished, "I was blown away." Then, in his prayer, Jesus sat down next to him in a deck chair and they talked as friends. This was a completely new experience for this pastor. He was deeply moved that Jesus was willing to meet him in a way that spoke so deeply to his own identity.

As we enter the story and allow it to unfold naturally, we can notice what is actually happening rather than what we think *should* happen. We may have a preconceived sense of a familiar story already formed in our minds. "Oh yeah," we might say, "Jesus in the storm. I know that one." What we mean is that we *know* the broad outlines of the story and the general lesson that it conveys. When we enter a story prayerfully, however, and allow it to unfold slowly, we may notice things that previously bypassed our senses. For example, in the storm story from Mark 4:35-41, you might notice that it is evening and growing dark. As your eyes adjust to the dim light you might notice that there are several boats sailing together, you might realize that the boat is quite small and crowded. As the storm begins to develop, perhaps you notice how the various characters in the boat respond. How do *you* respond? How do you feel as you listen to Jesus? Entering a story fills out these details so that we can deeply experience what is happening.

As a scene in a lived prayer experience unfolds you might be surprised by your responses. You might find yourself feeling things that do not fit your previous understanding of the story. Try to remain present to your emotions rather than editing or judging them or trying to explain or understand them. Our emotions have much to reveal to us. Remain curious and attentive. John Patton, a pastor and researcher, writes, "The process of learning to conceptualize gets in the way of seeing, hearing, and imagining what is going on around [us]."[7] Moving too quickly to analysis can be a way of deflecting strong emotions that accompany life experience. As you linger with your responses, what do they tell you about yourself? What do they reveal about your fear, trust, or confusion regarding Jesus? Rather than thinking about how we are *supposed* to view these stories, we need to listen deeply to them and notice what happens within us as we observe and encounter Jesus.

As you enter a story, consider which characters are intriguing to you. You might be Peter in his fishing boat or Mary sitting at the feet of Jesus. You might be a bystander in the crowd watching Jesus. You can observe from a distance or up close. If it is difficult to imagine a first century scene, you might create a modern equivalent to the biblical story. In Luke 5 when Jesus climbs onto Peter's boat while teaching the crowds, you might imagine Jesus coming into your office and holding a meeting in the over-crowded boardroom. You are not trying to imagine the *right* thing. You are hoping to notice what Jesus is actually doing and saying—and how you respond to him.

When I led a small group through a prayer experience with this story in Luke 5, one man imagined Jesus coming to his place of work and immediately noticed that he felt resistance to having Jesus there. He had been a Christian for many years and would not have described himself as resistant in this way, until he was faced with his actual response in prayer. This became an opportunity for him to pray through his responses and talk to Jesus about it.

When we relate to a particularly bold character, we may be longing to engage boldly with Jesus ourselves. Or we may find ourselves drawn to a character on the outskirts of the scene, who does not want to be noticed but wants to see Jesus. As we notice Jesus interacting with characters in a story, our work is to pay attention to what is happening within ourselves as the story unfolds.

---

7. Patton, *From Ministry to Theology*, 23.

JOURNALING OUR EXPERIENCE

When we journal about our imaginative prayer experience, we are able to slow down the action in a scene and create more space to notice our emotions and responses. Journaling can also help us to shift from simply observing a story to participating in it with our heart, mind, body, and soul. When we journal about a story, it becomes more deeply lodged in our memory because we have taken time to savor it and linger with it. I have heard many people say that after encountering Jesus in a particular story and taking time to journal about their experience, the memory of that encounter returns every time they read that story. Journaling can also give us space to ponder any questions that emerge during our imaginative prayer experience. These questions can lead us to further prayer times with the Lord.

After completing an imaginative prayer experience, take a few moments to recount what you are feeling in a prayer journal—what you heard and how you responded to Jesus as you talked together. It is important to journal even if the scene stopped prematurely, or you got distracted, or nothing seemed to happen. We can easily become discouraged in prayer but the presence of Jesus is always with us. We can ask him to reveal himself even when our prayer seems fruitless or comes to a dead end. In our prayer journals we can talk to Jesus about anything and everything that emerged for us through the story we were praying, sharing our frustrations, discouragements, and gratefulness for what we have received. If Jesus feels distant after a prayer journey, we can talk with him about that and tell him our desire to know him more personally.

A GROWING FRIENDSHIP

The prayer journey we will follow in the chapters ahead aligns roughly with the disciples' experience of getting to know Jesus and coming to a place of growing trust and love. As we pray this sequence of events, our longing is to grow in our own friendship with Jesus, just as we would with any person in our life as we live with them day by day. We begin curious because we don't know too much about our new friend. As we watch him and listen to him, we slowly begin to trust him with our hearts. We make decisions about how we can surrender our wills to his mysterious ways. As we continue to spend time with him, we become more responsive to his invitation to "lay down our lives" and follow him completely.

This process of slowly getting to know and trust Jesus and gradually responding to his invitation to follow him is often short circuited. If we have grown up in the faith, we have likely heard about Jesus and his call to "trust and obey" all of our lives. But no other relationships in our lives ask us to jump in and trust so quickly. In most relationships, our interest is piqued, our curiosity grows, and then vulnerability develops. Over time, love and intimacy emerge. When we pray slowly through the stories about Jesus, our friendship can grow more slowly and organically just as it does in the rest of our lives. The chapters that follow in Part II, "A Journey of Friendship," will explore this slowly developing dynamic.

As we embark on this journey of prayer, we invite the Spirit to give us "eyes to see and ears to hear" all that the Lord may want to give us as we travel. As we engage with Jesus through the stories in the Gospels, may we be surprised by powerful and deeply meaningful encounters with the One who fully knows us and completely loves us.

Let us begin by joining the young couple, Mary and Joseph, as they prepare to welcome Jesus into the world.

IMAGINATIVE PRAYER EXERCISE: JESUS' BIRTH (LUKE 2:4-7)[8]

Imagine yourself as a close friend to Mary and Joseph, perhaps a cousin or a neighbor. You have known them all your life. Yesterday, they asked you to accompany them as they travel to Bethlehem. You know about Caesar's decree but you're shocked that they'll be making this trip since Mary is pregnant. It may be very difficult for her. You see Mary over there gathering some things, talking to her mother and a neighbor. What do you notice about her?

You go to find Joseph. What do you say to him?

You look at a rough map with Joseph and figure you need to cover about 140 kilometers. You puzzle together about how far you can get each day. What supplies will you pack for this one-to-two-week journey? What emotions do you notice as you think about this trip?

---

8. This imagined reconstruction of the Gospel birth narrative has been influenced by Cyndi Parker and her book *Encountering Jesus in the Real World of the Gospels*. See especially pages 93–106. Through historical and textual research, Parker shows that the birth of Jesus would have looked more like the story imagined here than our modern "Christmas card" version.

The next day you all set out at first light. You are concerned because traveling is always dangerous, especially for women but there are a few people in your small company of travelers so that makes you feel a bit safer. You do feel anxious about getting to Bethlehem and back before this baby comes. As you walk together, imagine what you might say to your friends Mary and Joseph to encourage them. What would you want to ask them?

The days are long and hot. Imagine yourself walking slowly, sometimes talking, often silent, eating, sleeping, then moving again.

After many long days on the road, you finally arrive in Bethlehem. It is late and already dark. Joseph leads you to the relatives he knows live here. Surely they will take you in.

When you arrive you hear that other guests have already taken the spare room but there is space for Mary in the animal cave below the house. As you help Mary to settle in, what do you feel? How does Joseph respond? How does Mary respond?

Soon, you hear Mary moving about, groaning. The women from the household swarm her to assist in the birth and you move away to allow them room. Perhaps they invite you to help. Time seems to slow down as you see Mary moving about, trying to get comfortable. Time between contractions is shortening. It won't be long now.

You go to see Joseph. The men of the household are trying to talk to him, to reassure him. What do you notice about him? Your thoughts are interrupted by Mary's screams. You look at Joseph. He reaches for your hand.

The sounds intensify until . . . you hear the baby cry. What sensations do you feel?

When you are invited back into the cave you see the baby wrapped up tight. Mary is exhausted but her face radiates joy. You step closer to the manger where the baby lies. Do you reach out to touch him? Would you like to hold him?

Linger with Mary, Joseph, and the baby. Invite the Lord to bring to your mind whatever is important for you to see and feel.

When you are ready, close your time of prayer with thankfulness for your imagination and for the gift of this child.

PART II

A Journey of Friendship

We are now ready to set out on our journey. What we will discover is that praying with our imagination is a beautiful vehicle for the birth and growth of a friendship with Jesus. In fact, prayer as an activity begins to take a backseat to our real concern, which is a deeper connection and friendship with Jesus. As we make our way through the Gospels we will take the posture of those first disciples who were intrigued enough by Jesus to begin watching him more closely, listening to his words, and paying attention to all that he did and said. They went through various stages in their relationship with Jesus, just as any of us do when we first meet someone and begin a friendship. We will follow these stages as well, understanding that a relationship is a living thing, unique and personal to each of us. These stages are general seasons that we go through as a friendship grows and develops but we will always be surprised by the twists and turns that lie ahead.

CHAPTER 4

Watching Jesus

One thing I ask from the Lord, this only do I seek:
that I may dwell in the house of the Lord all the days of my life,
to gaze upon the beauty of the Lord
and to seek him in his temple.

My heart says of you, "Seek his face!"
Your face, Lord, I will seek!

—Psalm 27:4, 8

I STILL REMEMBER THE first time I saw my wife Andrea. Tim and I were visiting a church in Brisbane, Australia for a Sunday evening service. As a few of us mingled around beforehand, she swept in with her long, curly, stunning red hair, infectious laugh, and a mischievous twinkle in her eye. I did not meet her right away but saw her greet her family and then sit down near the back of the church. Tim was sitting directly in front of her and they were soon chatting away, laughing, swapping stories. I was intrigued—not yet smitten, but I soon would be. These initial glimpses compelled me to want to talk with her and get to know her.

We can pick up lots of information about people simply by watching how they talk to others, how they carry themselves, the kind of "vibe" they emanate. As we begin our prayer journey, we will be watching Jesus as he is baptized in the river, teaches in the synagogue, and begins his ministry around Galilee. We will be like citizens of the small towns of Israel who observed this new rabbi and miracle worker. We will pay attention to how we respond to this person who so readily invites people to "follow me." Perhaps you remember the first time you were captivated by these Gospel stories. Perhaps you imagined what it would have been like to be there and see Jesus yourself. This is what imaginative prayer offers us.

As we gain more familiarity with these Gospel stories in our Christian lives, our emphasis tends to shift away from that initial captivated interest toward a posture of *learning*. We look for lessons and principles beneath the stories, mining them for models of behavior or instructions on how to live as Christians. Though it is important to learn how these stories fit into the larger narrative of how God works with his people, we can begin to lose sight of Jesus as a person in the midst of all the "lessons." Jesus becomes the abstract subject of a spiritual message rather than an actual person to encounter. We may find ourselves "trying to love an ideal and be loyal to a principle"[1] rather than engage with Jesus personally.

As we begin our journey of prayer, I invite you to return to the simple act of watching Jesus as he goes about his life in the Gospels, entering these stories as if you are there. Nearly everyone in the Gospels had already *heard* of Jesus before they encountered him. They might have seen him down by the river getting baptized, or they might have heard him preach in the synagogue. Intrigued, they followed the crowds that formed around him. They witnessed some of his miracles. They noticed how he talked to people. Perhaps they even heard him teaching up close, at a dinner party, on a street corner, in a garden. When we first enter into the Gospel stories through our imagination, we observe Jesus like those first disciples, like I watched Andrea that first Sunday evening, and we allow ourselves to be drawn in.

OBSERVING UP CLOSE

While most of us are well-practiced at observing Jesus from a distance as we read or listen to a Gospel story, we typically do not think of our watching as prayer. But when we prayerfully observe Jesus through our imaginations, we deliberately draw close to him, watching him much more carefully. When we do this, the stories begin to come to life, and we find ourselves wanting to see even more.

I once had a New Testament professor who began every course he taught with his favorite story from his seminary days. His professor brought

1. Tozer, *Pursuit of God*, 50.

in a fish, plopped it on the table at the front of the class, and said, "Look at the fish and write down everything you see." Then he left. The students gathered around and spent the entire class period jotting down every possible thing they could see in that fish. The next day, the professor brought in the fish again. "Look at the fish!" he said, and off he went. The students dutifully gathered around the fish and looked intently at it. To their surprise, they saw things they had not noticed on the first day. On the third day of class, once again, the professor brought in the fish and said, "Look at the fish." Many thought this was ridiculous, but as they spent time looking, even finer details emerged. The professor was teaching the class to slow down and pay attention.[2] Imaginative prayer ushers us into this same kind of careful attentiveness. We enter into the Gospel stories and pay attention to what we see and what we notice as we prayerfully watch Jesus.

When we enter these stories imaginatively, we may notice many fascinating details that we would miss if we simply read the stories as "lessons." For example, we might notice that it would be a long time for Jesus and his disciples to walk from Bethany to Jerusalem which might lead us to wonder what happened as they walked along. What did they talk about? What did the disciples notice about Jesus over a long walk like this? The disciples' ability to listen to and eventually trust Jesus was honed over many such walks as this. We have similar needs. Our relationships also need this kind of slow, careful observation of the one who has caught our attention. The details we see in our friends are the things that add to our attraction.

As we embark on this imaginative prayer journey, we will discover that the dynamics present in our other relationships are often mirrored in our developing relationship with Jesus. Prayerfully attending to these relational stages can help our relationship with Jesus grow more naturally.

LOOKING BEFORE WE LEAP

When I was young and hearing the Gospel stories for the first time, I imagined Jesus coming up to people on the street—total strangers—and telling them to follow him. And they would. Just like that! This caused me a lot of turmoil. I wondered how anybody could simply drop everything to follow Jesus. These eager disciples were lauded as great men and women of faith, willing to follow Jesus at the drop of a hat. The not-so-subtle message I

2. Upon researching the origin of this story, I discovered that my professor might have been borrowing this story from others. The origin is unclear.

heard was that I should be willing to do that as well, but I knew I was a long way from that. I internalized this "drop everything and follow" discipleship as a picture of *real* faith and trust in Jesus. But if this is what real believers did, I didn't know where that left me. Later in my life, as I began to pray with these stories and imagine Jesus walking up to me in this way, the deep angst I had felt as a young person only intensified. I could feel my resistance to responding in this "drop everything" sort of way.

Then I began to imagine what it would be like to experience this "drop everything" attitude in my actual life. What if someone I've never met or heard of walked up to me at work or in the grocery store and said, "Follow me," then turned and walked away. Would I go? Of course not! You wouldn't either—and most importantly, you would not feel guilty about it. You would think it extremely odd if *anyone* followed somebody in that scenario. You would want to know who this person was, what he wanted from you, what his character was like, if he could be trusted. Actually, you would probably be happy to have him walk away and leave you alone. I do not think the people in the first century were much different. They were not inherently more trusting than us. If they were the slightest bit intrigued, perhaps because the person was a local celebrity, they would still want to know more about them before they made any commitment to follow them. I think that is exactly what happened in the Gospels.

When we look closely at these Gospel stories and enter into them prayerfully, we can recognize that most of the early followers of Jesus did not respond in such a radical way. Most had already heard about Jesus and seen him around town, teaching and performing miracles. Those who followed him had already been watching him. Luke tells us early in his Gospel that after Jesus was baptized and spent forty days in the desert, he began his public ministry. Before Luke tells us about anyone following Jesus, he writes, "Jesus returned to Galilee in the power of the Spirit, and *news about him spread throughout the whole countryside.*" (Luke 4:14, emphasis added). Jesus was becoming famous and gaining a reputation. People were likely forming opinions about him and talking about him with their friends.

Similarly, when Levi, the tax collector, is called by Jesus, it might seem as if Levi simply drops everything and follows Jesus (Luke 5:27–28). But was this the first time Levi had ever seen Jesus? Earlier in Luke, we see Jesus performing many miracles—driving out demons, healing a man with leprosy, healing the paralytic lowered through the roof. Might Levi have been a witness to some or all of these events? These towns where Jesus ministered were small and it is reasonable to assume that everyone would know of the miracle-working rabbi who was making the rounds.

What would you think and feel if you saw Jesus performing these miracles and "teaching with authority"? You would probably be amazed and intrigued! By the time Jesus approaches Levi and asks him to follow, Levi had probably been watching Jesus for some time. Though we are not explicitly told this in Scripture, these details emerge when we enter the stories imaginatively and experience the events as they might have unfolded. Our imaginations can place us much closer to the first followers of Jesus, who wondered, questioned, and doubted—just as we do. As amazing as it was for Levi to "drop everything and follow," you might have done the same if you had seen everything that he had seen. When I first noticed this in prayer, it was beautifully freeing. I realized I had time to simply watch Jesus and find out a bit about him before I "dropped everything and followed."

Before we begin, we need to, as best we can, lay aside everything we already know about Jesus so that we can notice him afresh, just like the first disciples. Those of us who have been Christians for a long time will need to imagine that we have never seen or met him before. Obviously, we cannot "unknow" what we already know, but we can do our best to imagine ourselves standing with the crowds in Galilee, Nazareth, and Jerusalem as they watch and listen to this itinerant preacher and miracle-worker. Though we might think we have already seen everything there is to see in Jesus, we need to "look at the fish" again with fresh eyes.

We will pause here and enter into prayer. Each chapter in Part II will include two guided prayer exercises to usher you into Gospel stories that embody the various stages of your developing relationship with Jesus. They can all be found in audio format at www.danheavenor.com. For each exercise, try to find a quiet place to pray. Relax and invite the Spirit to animate your imagination and lead you into the story. My descriptions of the stories are intended as a simple guide. As you live into a story your imagination may lead you in different directions. If this happens, simply follow the narrative that actually emerges for you, trusting the Spirit to be your guide.

IMAGINATIVE PRAYER EXERCISE: THE SYNAGOGUE (LUKE 4:14–22)

In Luke 4, Luke tells us that Jesus went from Galilee to Nazareth, "where he had been brought up" (4:16). From this small detail, we can assume that everyone in Nazareth knew Jesus from birth. He was simply one of the local boys who had grown up there.

~

You live in the small town of Nazareth. It is the Sabbath, and you have made your way to the synagogue for worship. You enter the synagogue, chat with some friends who are standing near the entrance and make your way toward a place to sit. As you look around, linger briefly on the faces you recognize. You realize that you know almost everyone. More people arrive, sit, and ready themselves. What do you notice about the people around you? Across the room, you see a young man you think you recognize. You nudge your neighbor. "Isn't that Jesus, Joseph and Mary's son, over there?"

Then Jesus stands, walks to the front, and receives the scroll for the reading. A hush comes over the group. "The Spirit of the Lord is upon me," he reads, "because he has anointed me to preach the good news." You recognize the passage—Isaiah 61—as one of your favorites with all the prophecies about the Messiah who will come and rescue your people. This reminds you of the Roman soldiers who hassled you yesterday. "Oh, Lord," you pray silently to yourself, "free us from these wretched Romans!" When Jesus finishes reading, he hands the scroll back to the rabbi. As everyone watches him and waits, the silence in the room grows heavy. You wonder what Jesus might say. You try to remember what the rabbis usually say about this passage.

Then Jesus says, "Today this scripture is fulfilled in your hearing."

You could hear a pin drop. You wonder what this son of Joseph, a local carpenter from across town, is saying? What do his words stir in you? How do they make you feel? How are the people around you responding? What does Jesus do next?

ATTENDING TO WHAT YOU NOTICE

Lectio divina is an ancient prayer practice where one reads a short passage of Scripture and pays attention to any word or phrase that jumps out at you asking for your attention. We are doing the same in Gospel stories, entering in imaginatively and paying close attention to any detail in the scene that catches your attention. Perhaps you notice something you have never noticed before, even though you have read the passage many times.

Pay close attention to these moments, What is drawing you into the scene? How are your emotions stirred? Rather than trying to figure things out in a cognitive way, allow the scene to speak as it unfolds before you. Invite the Spirit to help you notice what God has for you. Trust that God is present in all the simple details.

As you watch a story unfold, what do you notice about Jesus? What is his attitude? How does he speak? How does he treat people? By watching Jesus, we learn to pay attention to *him* first, instead of rushing to *our* experience, *our* needs, *our* requests, or *our* confession of sin. Our responses and emotions are worth paying attention to. They are important and not to be discarded. But watching Jesus as we begin our journey is a way to keep our eyes and attention centered on him. When we spend time watching Jesus, we see that God is always acting before we ever arrive on the scene.

Some years ago there was a movie about Jesus that played on network television. Every few years a filmmaker attempts to bring the stories in the Gospels to life by portraying scenes from Scripture as they might have actually happened. They do a wonderful job of helping viewers imagine what it might have been like to live in Jesus' day and to see him interact with people. It is just this kind of *seeing* that we do in imaginative prayer. In one particularly memorable scene, Jesus is walking down a village street with several of his disciples, talking and laughing together. Along the side of the road, a waist-high cylindrical stone table with a slight dip in the center has gathered water. The table catches Jesus' attention and as he passes it he reaches out his hand and flicks water at the disciples walking behind him. He grins a joyful grin and runs off as his friends chase him, wiping the water from their faces and laughing. This simple, human gesture spoke to me deeply. Though Jesus taught in the synagogues and healed people from their diseases, he also talked and laughed and joked with his friends. All my years of learning *lessons* from Bible stories had removed me from this very *human* Jesus, a man who laughed with his friends.

Because the Gospel writers were concerned with telling the story of Jesus as the Messiah of Israel—the healer, teacher, and Lord of the Kingdom—they did not include simple details from everyday life unless they held some significance for the story. While modern novels and stories include these kinds of details, the literature of that time was not concerned with the minutiae of everyday life. Our lives, though, are made up of thousands of small details like this. We experience life through thousands of small moments rather than grandiose narrative arcs. If Jesus only inhabits a large narrative, it can be difficult to find him in the reality of my day-to-day existence. When we enter into these stories in prayer, our imaginations can populate the scene with the details of real life as we experience it, helping us see Jesus living an actual human life.

I once had my own experience in prayer where this was brought to life for me. I wanted to pray with the story of the rich young ruler in Matthew 19, which begins, "And then a man came up to Jesus and asked . . ." (v. 16). To ease myself into the scene, I wondered what this man might have been doing immediately prior to this episode. I looked earlier in the text for any clues. In the story immediately preceding this text (in Matthew as well as Mark and Luke), children are brought to Jesus to receive a blessing. This would be the place I would prayerfully enter the story. I imagined myself as a man waiting to speak with Jesus. I placed myself standing on a slight rise alongside a road of a small village. I was several feet away from Jesus, waiting for my opportunity to approach him. As I read, "Then little children were brought to Jesus for him to place his hand on them and pray for them," I imagined all these kids roaming around, laughing, and climbing onto Jesus' back, clutching his neck. I was amazed and touched by Jesus' unabashed joy. His laugh was infectious. He rustled one boy's hair, tickled a little girl on her arm, bent down to look a toddler in the eyes, and took a crying baby into his arms, blessing each child with his warmth and tenderness (Mark 10:16). I saw Jesus pretend to fall over and all the kids piled on top of him as he laughed and rolled around on the ground, tickling anyone within reach. Then he leapt up and swung two youngsters off his back and bent down to kiss a little girl that was hugging his leg. As I watched Jesus interact with all these children, tears began streaming down my face. I had never imagined Jesus like this, playing with such delight and joy. I had grown up hearing that Jesus loved me but I had never imagined what that love *looked* like.

If Jesus had been overly serious and austere, concerned only with "adult" things then kids would have likely stayed away, but they were obviously drawn to Jesus. They could see that he was safe and loving, fun and filled with joy. Jesus was attractive to sinners and tax collectors, prostitutes and outcasts, children, and lepers because he exuded joy rather than condemnation. If the kingdom of God *belongs* to the little children (Luke 18:16), then the king of that kingdom will be down on his knees, looking them in the eye, laughing with them, and welcoming them into his kingdom with open arms. I might have been able to think theologically about

God's love and joy, but seeing Jesus laughing and playing with children opened my heart to him in new ways.

Since this imaginative prayer encounter, Jesus' smile and laughter have become an important part of my life. I can tend to hear scriptural truths about God's love conceptually and metaphorically while missing the *experience* of those truths. As Brian Edgar insightfully observes, "God engages in a playful relationship with his people," so that, "the freedom, creativity, and the integrity of each person is affirmed and enhanced."[3] I was so moved by this scene of Jesus playing with the little children that I never got to the story of the rich young ruler. God had something different in mind for me that day.

When we pray imaginatively, we are often brought up short by the compassion, joy, and tenderness we notice in Jesus. These experiences can have a tremendous impact on our ability to trust God, to move closer to Jesus, and to open our hearts to him.

IMAGINATIVE PRAYER EXERCISE: THE BAPTISM OF JESUS (MATT 3:1–17)

You are in your small village near Jerusalem when you hear that a man whom some are calling a prophet is preaching and baptizing people in the Jordan river. You join others in your family who are setting out to hear him teach. On the walk to the river, you start to wonder about the rumors. *A prophet?* You wonder. There has not been a prophet in Israel for hundreds of years! As you continue to walk towards the river, what are you thinking about? What are you feeling? What do you hear others saying?

As you approach the river, you see a crowd gathered along the bank. You hear a loud voice bellowing above the crowd. As you get closer, you begin to make out the words: "Repent, for the kingdom of heaven is near."

What images come to mind as you hear this?

You find a place to sit on the slope where you have a good view. The prophet, "John" someone tells you, is standing in the river, the water half-way up his legs. He is a strange looking man, wearing camel hair clothes and a leather belt. His hair and beard are thick, black, and wild. His eyes are intense and focused on the people who are lined up, waiting to enter the water. You notice several others who are soaking wet, sitting on the shore, listening with rapt attention.

3. Edgar, *God Who Plays*, 46.

Where are your eyes drawn? What do you notice about the landscape or the people around you?

Then the prophet steps toward a group of priests standing near the shoreline.

"You brood of vipers!" he yells. "Who warned you to flee from the coming wrath? Produce fruit in keeping with repentance. And do not think you can say to yourselves, 'We have Abraham as our father.' I tell you that out of these stones God can raise up children for Abraham. The ax is already at the root of the trees, and every tree that does not produce good fruit will be cut down and thrown into the fire."

These words unsettle you. You have never heard anyone preach like this before. You look around and notice people with tears in their eyes. As you see more and more people getting in line to be baptized, what stirs within you?

Turning away from the priests, the prophet faces the crowd and says, "I baptize you with water for repentance. But after me comes one who is more powerful than I, whose sandals I am not worthy to carry. He will baptize you with the Holy Spirit and with fire."

You wonder who this "powerful one" could possibly be? You hear others in the crowd murmuring to one another, repeating these bewildering words in fierce whispers.

Then you notice a slight commotion near the back of the crowd. People are shifting to make way for someone. A man you don't recognize walks down to the river's edge and enters the water. The prophet looks directly at the man with an expression of stunned recognition. Then the prophet says something you cannot hear. As the two men speak quietly to one another in the water, you strain to hear their words.

"I need to be baptized by you," John says, "and do you come to me?"

The conversation continues for a few moments. Then you hear the stranger say, "Let it be so now; it is proper for us to do this to fulfill all righteousness." There is a long pause. Finally John lowers his head and baptizes the stranger.

As soon as the man comes up out of the water, a shaft of light pours down from the heavens, brightly illuminating his head and the surface of the water. Then a bird, a dove, descends and gently lands on the man's head. You feel a twinge of fear as a voice that seems to be coming from the clouds says, "This is my Son, whom I love; with him I am well pleased."

What do you notice about the stranger as you hear these words? What emotions do these words stir within you? Remain here for a few minutes. Can you imagine the Father saying these words to you? "You, my son, my daughter, you are my beloved."

As the scene fades, remain with Jesus and talk to him about this experience. What questions arise for you? What feelings are surfacing that you want to explore with Jesus?

CHAPTER 5

Meeting Jesus

That which was from the beginning,
which we have heard, which we have seen with our eyes,
which we have looked at and our hands have touched . . .
We proclaim to you what we have seen and heard.

—1 John 1:1–3

THINK BACK TO WHEN you first met a good friend. Chances are you can remember many details about that meeting, where you were, how old you were, what was going on in your life, maybe even what you were wearing. I still have a picture in my mind of first meeting Dave at Kits Beach in Vancouver. The meeting had been set up by a colleague of mine. He thought I should meet Dave. When I did, sitting on the beach on a warm spring day with our jeans rolled up the conversation sprang to life and rolled along easily. We swapped stories and laughed at each other's jokes. The memory is well formed in my mind, perhaps because Dave is one of my best friends. That meeting was over twenty-five years ago.

If you could ask Peter, Zacchaeus, or the Samaritan woman at the well if they had met Jesus, they would all respond with a resounding "Yes!" Each could likely recount in fine detail what it was like to meet him, what he said to them, how it felt to be in his presence. But when *we* think about meeting Jesus, if you are anything like me, you grow awkwardly silent. Your own certainty about whether you've met Jesus might not be so obvious. You may feel a little uncomfortable about this. You're supposed to be able to say, "Of course I've met Jesus. I am a Christian!" But when you stop to think about it, compared with other people you've met in your life, it is an awkward question. You may identify yourself as a Christian. You may be able to recite the Apostles' Creed and the Lord's Prayer. You may even be engaged in ministry in some way. But have you *met* Jesus?

Even though I had thought of myself as a Christian for many years I found it difficult to know if I had actually met Jesus. I prayed. I tried to learn about Jesus by reading and studying the Bible. I trusted his forgiveness. I believed in the resurrection. But had I *met* him? For a long time this question left me at a loss for words. But as I began to face this question more honestly, a deep desire to *meet* Jesus, began to awaken in me, and I found myself longing to enter into a relationship that felt more real.

By this time in my life I had studied theology and been in ministry for a number of years. This question about meeting Jesus had never been central in any of my studies or ministry activities. The predominant focus had been on learning the story of Scripture and applying that to my life. But as one theologian writes, "It is futile to leaf through the writings of the Old and New covenant in the hopes of coming across truths of one kind or another, unless we are prepared to be exposed to a direct encounter with him, the personal, utterly free Word which makes severe claims upon us."[1] Throughout Scripture, God comes directly to people and meets them, speaks to them, warns them, weeps over them. The people listen to him, resist him, and yield to him. They are not yielding to an idea or a set of principles but are having an encounter with a person.

Many of us remain in the *watching* stage with Jesus for a long time, perhaps even for a lifetime. We can gain many benefits from watching and learning from Jesus, as we saw in the last chapter, but if we remain there Jesus will seem remote and beyond reach. He will remain a historical figure or the embodiment of a set of beliefs, ideals, or principles rather than someone with whom we can relate in a loving way. The relational words "follow," "trust," and "love" will have little experiential reality for us in our life with God. We have become adept at using relational language in regard to God but when we compare this language with our actual experience a great vacuum seems to open up within us.

For many years I struggled to know what *trusting* and *loving* God actually looked like in my life. Could I love God by adhering to a set of beliefs? Was I trusting God when I aligned myself with certain behaviors? In all my

---

1. von Balthasar, *Prayer*, 18–19.

other relationships, I experienced love and trust much more viscerally but my faith relationship with God seemed overly cognitive. How was being a Christian any different from adhering to some set of philosophical ideals? As A.W. Tozer puts it, I was "substituting theological ideas for an arresting encounter"[2] with Jesus. I began to wrestle with the nature of my actual relationship with God. Could I even describe it as a *relationship*? Eventually, the relational language I was using felt more and more hollow and I began to wonder if I had ever really *met* the person who stood at the center of the whole story. My heart felt completely empty.

As I entered into imaginative prayer, the Lord met me as I wrestled with these questions. When I prayerfully enter a Gospel story, placing myself in the crowd, watching and listening to Jesus, I slowly move beyond philosophical ideals into the realm of encounter. When Jesus suddenly turns and looks at me or calls me by name, I am jolted from being a passive observer to an active participant. When we are the one approaching Jesus covered with our own form of leprosy and Jesus looks us in the eyes, lays his hands on our diseased body, and heals us, we move beyond cognitive speculations and fall at his feet in worship. You are invited now to come and *meet* him.

LET ME INTRODUCE YOU

If we remain in a watching posture toward Jesus, as helpful as that can be, eventually it can begin to feel like we are relating to a celebrity. We can know a lot about celebrities, see all their movies, read all their books, listen to all their interviews, but we do not have a relationship with them. If a celebrity were to show up at your door one day and introduce themselves, your connection to them would be completely transformed. Meeting them in person and having a conversation would be utterly different from your previous experience. You might have done tons of research and even accumulated rare footage of this celebrity that no one else had seen before. You might have felt qualified to write about them, peppering your stories with previously unknown facts. As amazing as all this knowledge would be, it would pale in comparison to actually *meeting* this person. Imagine Matt Damon showing up at work one day and asking you out for lunch. Or imagine opening your front door and seeing Taylor Swift standing there. It would probably feel like all you had learned about this person up to this

2. Tozer, quoted in Benner, *Surrender to Love,* 27.

point was hardly worth knowing. You would be catapulted into an entirely new reality with them.[3]

While it might be hard to admit that we relate to Jesus like we relate to celebrities, the truth is, for many of us, this is exactly what our relationship with Jesus feels like. We may know all kinds of things about Jesus, can quote many Bible verses and pass any knowledge exam but we know deep down that we have never actually *met* him. We may have had an initial encounter that drew us into faith but an ongoing relationship with him as a real person seems to elude us. We find ourselves sitting in the crowd with other Christians, watching, listening, learning, trying to obey, but uncertain if we have truly met him.

When we first begin imaginative prayer we often perceive ourselves to be at a bit of a distance from Jesus. We see him standing there, talking, listening, but we are still strangers to him. In our particular spirituality we may use the language of *relationship* yet when we stand on the street with Jesus or watch him in the synagogue we may wonder about the validity of using this word. We may affirm that we "have Jesus in our heart" or that we "trust Jesus with our life," but after watching Jesus in imaginative prayer we recognize a growing desire to truly *meet* this person who is captivating us.

Lesslie Newbiggin, the long-time missionary to India, aptly described the incarnation of Jesus as two friends speaking about a third friend when suddenly, the third friend walks into the room.[4] Picture that moment. Something important has happened. The conversation cannot remain the same once the third friend appears. I spent many years of my Christian life as one of the "two friends" talking about Jesus. Theologically, I believed he had "walked into the room," but I had rarely experienced it. I simply continued talking *about* him. The more I prayed with my imagination, the more I felt invited to engage this "third friend" in conversation and relationship.

When we enter the stories of the Gospels and spend time watching and listening to Jesus, we begin to recognize a burning desire to meet him ourselves. We become less and less satisfied when we hear other people tell their stories of meeting Jesus. We have remained at a safe distance long enough. It is time to introduce ourselves.

3. Historians say that Thomas Aquinas had an experience much like this. After a profound encounter with the Lord near the end of his life he purportedly said, "Everything I have written seems like straw compared to those things that I have seen and have been revealed to me." See Sanders, "Thomas Aquinas' Big Pile of Straw."

4. I heard this story from Lesslie Newbiggin on a recorded sermon, the title of which I have long since forgotten.

JESUS GATHERS FRIENDS

In the early chapters of the Gospels we see Jesus befriending individual people. He might not have done this. He might have remained an itinerant preacher to faceless crowds or performed healings and miracles for unnamed individuals but Jesus meets real people and forms relationships with them. He makes friends. As a human being this is not extraordinary. We all do this. But when we understand that Jesus is a revelation of God, this is spectacular and surprising! We are not left to relate to an impersonal Other, the Mystery Beyond, or Ineffable Light. We are each invited to meet a person who has a name—and who wants to know *us* by name.

The Gospel of John is particularly interested in the way Jesus meets and gathers his friends around him. In his very first chapter, John recounts how Jesus meets Andrew, his brother Peter, Philip and his friend, Nathaniel (John 1:35–51), inviting each one into friendship. These are all very human encounters, each with a particular and unique set of circumstances surrounding them. But they are not chance encounters. Jesus makes clear that he has *chosen* these people to be his friends. He tells them later, "You did not choose me, but I chose you" (John 15:16). Jesus finds and calls specific people who will be his closest friends, living life with him and assisting him in his mission. Jesus reveals a God who wants to meet us face to face, call us by name, and invite us into an ongoing relationship.

IMAGINATIVE PRAYER EXERCISE: JESUS LOOKS AT YOU (LUKE 19:1-9)

Imagine that you are living alone in a small town where everyone knows everyone else. For you, this is not a good thing because you are despised in this town. When you go out into the market, people move away from you, whisper behind your back, and cross the road to avoid you. It has been this way for years. You are used to it, but it still hurts.

What does it feel like to live this way?

Today, now, you are in your small house, cleaning up, and you hear a faint, dull sound. You listen, but it seems to fade, and so you return to your work. Then you hear it again, a bit louder. It is a dim but growing roar that is getting closer. You move to the front of the house, curious. As you listen to this sound, how do you feel? What thoughts are racing through your mind?

As the sound grows steadily louder and closer, you peer out the window but you can't see anything. You walk to the door and open it. The noise escalates but you still cannot see what is causing it. You cautiously move towards the edge of the street and look down the road.

What details do you notice about the street?

As you look far down the road, you see the shape of a large crowd moving toward you. Are they coming for you? You grow tense, fearful of what they might do to you or your house.

As you watch and listen to the approaching crowd, you notice that it is not an angry crowd, but . . . joyous. You hear people laughing, shouting, talking, calling out. As they grow closer, you notice someone in the center of the group. People are walking alongside this person, pressing against him from all sides. Some people in the front of the crowd are walking backwards, their eyes fixed on him. Others are leaping up from the side of the crowd as if trying to get a better glimpse of him.

Then you hear people yelling, "Jesus, Jesus!"

You have heard this name before. You have heard stories about this man's power to heal, of miracles, and amazing teaching. You have been intrigued, but you know that such a man would have nothing to do with you. He would look at you as everyone looks at you, with derision and contempt.

Yet something deep within you compels you to see what this man looks like.

As the crowd draws closer, you glance around and see a sycamore tree. You quickly decide to climb into the tree so you can see the man without being noticed. You race to the tree and climb as high as you can.

What do you notice from this new height?

It has been many years since you climbed a tree. You suddenly remember climbing trees as a child, back when people still included you and called you friend.

How does it feel to remember this time in your life? Do you have other memories of times before you started to carry this shame?

As the crowd approaches the tree, you are relieved that no one notices you. The crowd parts to move around the tree but the man in the center, whom you now know is Jesus, stops.

A hush moves through the crowd.

What do you feel? Can you feel your heart racing?

Then Jesus looks up. Your eyes meet. There is utter silence as people wait to hear what he will say. What do you feel as he looks at you?

Then he says your name.

"Come down, my friend. I must stay at your house today."

As the crowd begins to mutter, you continue to hear the echo of your name on his lips and to feel his eyes holding your gaze.

What do you feel right now? How do you want to respond to Jesus?

Linger in the tree for a moment. Pay attention to what you see and hear.

Now jump down from the tree and begin to escort Jesus back into your house. Do you say anything to him? What does Jesus say to you? What questions do you want to ask him? What emotions are rising up in you? Can you share these with Jesus? How does he respond?

EXPERIENCING JESUS

It is our *experience* with others that is the bedrock of any relationship. Relationships require shared personal experience in order to grow and flourish. Simply thinking about someone is not enough to sustain a friendship. We are far more than simply minds that think. We are bodies that collect and store experiences. It is this firsthand experience that forms the foundation of friendship and shapes us into the people we are and are becoming. This is true in our relationship with Jesus as well. Once we meet him, we begin to desire face to face interaction in order to form the relationship we long for.

When the residents of Sychar in John 4 heard about Jesus from the woman at the well they were intrigued, even moved. Some believed in Jesus based on her testimony, we are told, but many others wanted to meet and listen to Jesus themselves. They were not content with secondhand knowledge. "We no longer believe just because of what you said; now we have heard for ourselves" (John 4:42). How many of us resonate with this longing to meet Jesus ourselves? Though we have heard others talk about him, our knowledge has remained secondhand. Similarly, after Job listens to and argues with his friends about God (for thirty-seven chapters!), he is finally confronted by the Lord himself. He had been mostly talking *about* God. Now he experiences the personal reality *of* God and he is undone. "My ears had heard of you but now my eyes have seen you" (Job 42:5 NIV). Though he already knew all about God and had lived all of his life loving and worshiping God, now he has *met* him. This is a profoundly new experience.

Several years ago, I had an email conversation with a pastor who was troubled by my longing to experience God. In exasperation, he wrote,

"Scripture does not teach us to experience God but to trust God!" I whole-heartedly agree that the Bible teaches us to trust God but how can we pos-sibly come to know and trust God if we have never met him? The Bible recounts the experience of encountering God on nearly every page. It tells us to "seek him" with all of our hearts, which implies an actual lived expe-rience of God when we find him. Can we deeply trust someone we have never met? Don't we have to experience God in order to trust him?

The Bible itself is a product of experience. Knowledge about God did not emerge out of thin air. It began in personal experience. Adam and Eve relate to and talk to God personally in the early pages of Genesis. Abram hears God calling him to leave his country and follow. He does not find some ancient manuscript of proverbs, nor does he attempt to meditate him-self into some kind of spiritual nirvana. He hears a voice and has a personal encounter. Then he passes down these stories about God to his children and grandchildren and eventually they are written down and passed on to us.

Moses sees the burning bush and hears God speak to him on Mt. Sinai. Later, he sets up a tent where he sits and speaks with God, "face to face, as one speaks to his friend" (Exodus 33:11). The name of this tent? The Tent of Meeting! Later, the prophets meet with God, hear God speak—often with the use of bizarre and fantastic symbols and imagery—and then relay what they have heard and experienced to the people.

Finally, as if to punctuate this reality, God himself, "became flesh and blood and moved into the neighborhood," as Eugene Peterson dynamically describes the incarnation (John 1:14, *The Message*). Jesus came to allow us to experience him in the flesh. It is this experience of Jesus that became the foundation of the four Gospels. As John writes in his first epistle, "We proclaim to you what we have seen and heard" (1 John 1:3). William Barry and William Connolly, two Jesuit priests and spiritual directors, write, "The apostles came to believe in Jesus and to trust in him through their experi-ence of him. A great deal of thought about Jesus has resulted from their experience, but the basis for the thought was the experience itself."[5] The disciples' faith and love for Jesus did not come about through thinking or theorizing—they *experienced* a relationship with a real person.

Others also wrote about their experiences of God to pass on to the community of faith. Paul encountered Jesus on the road to Damascus and experienced the power of the Holy Spirit speaking to him and empowering

5. Barry and Connolly, *Practice of Spiritual Direction*, 22.

him for ministry. The early Christians experienced the Spirit's presence in their midst through amazing gifts and abilities. And the Bible ends with John's revelation—a profoundly experiential vision that he had on the island of Patmos. Personal human experience is central to the revelation of God and the claims of the gospel, promising that we can have a relationship of love with God. We can trust and rely on a personal God who relates to us through our experiences.

Plain and simple, God desires to meet us. He presents himself as one who can be experienced in our lives, in particular and recognizable ways. Our faith is not merely a cognitive exercise of believing certain truths. It is a relationship of abiding trust in the One who *is* truth. The Bible itself would not exist if people throughout history had not had a deeply personal experience of God.

Obviously, we can no longer meet Jesus on the street and hear his invitation to follow him, as the first disciples did, but through our imagination we can experience Jesus in tangible ways that work to strengthen our trust and deepen our love for him.

"YOU HAD TO BE THERE"

Author and Christian historian Philip Sheldrake says that when we pray with our imagination, "it gives [us] a sense of the experience very like actually, bodily experiencing it which has a decidedly different character than simply thinking about something."[6] This "decidedly different character" is a deep and personal connection which we understand intuitively when we say, "You just had to be there" to someone who cannot grasp what we are trying to describe with words.

We cannot experience this sense of "being there" through cognitive processes alone. Mark Twain highlights the difference between cognitive and experiential knowledge with the quip, "He who carries a cat by the tail learns something he can learn in no other way."[7] Your mind is probably already at work trying to imagine that scenario! Obviously, *talking* or *hearing* about an experience is quite different from actually living it. As James K.A. Smith writes, "There is an irreducible know-how 'carried' in the experience itself . . . I learn something in the doing that can't ever be put into words and

6. Sheldrake, "Imagination and Prayer," 101.
7. Quoted in Smith, *You Are What You Love,* 85.

yet it is its own irreducible sort of understanding."[8] When we prayerfully imagine ourselves into Jesus' life in the Gospels, we receive this kind of "irreducible" understanding, which can be difficult to express with words. We might well revert to "You just had to be there."

When we watch a riveting movie or read a captivating novel, our heart begins to pound and we find ourselves moved to tears or roused to anger. How can words on a page or pixels on a screen trigger such deep emotional responses? Our imagination has kicked into gear. Our imaginations are activating these responses *as if* the actions were actually occurring in real life. Our imaginations move us from being spectators and observers to being active participants in the story. Similarly, when we prayerfully enter Gospel stories with our imagination, we become active participants in the life of Jesus.

When our only experience of prayer is conceptual or systematic, we can avoid or bury our deeply rooted feelings, memories, and honest responses. We might pray for all kinds of things yet feel disconnected from our words, as if they are spilling out of our mouth and falling to the ground. Before I began to pray with my imagination, I often wondered if my prayers were nothing more than thoughts in my head. There was nothing *relational* about these prayers and I certainly did not feel much emotional connection to what I was saying—nor that anyone was actually listening. Imaginative prayer has helped move me beyond mere thoughts and words to actual experiences, often uncovering uncomfortable and vulnerable areas within me that God wants to heal. When we allow these vulnerabilities to surface, inviting Jesus to be present to us in all that we are feeling and experiencing, we open ourselves to a more holistic relationship with God.

Imagine that you are sad or deeply grieving. A friend asks you how you are feeling and you respond by saying a perfunctory, "I'm fine." This is a rational response. All things considered, you feel sad but not overwhelmed. You'll get over it. But then your friend approaches you and embraces you. You find yourself crumbling into their arms, weeping. You are no longer able to keep the emotion at bay. The physical experience of being touched and embraced has reconnected you to your true emotions. In the safety of that embrace you are able to allow your true emotions to emerge. The thinking self, in response to the conceptual question, responds with a conceptual answer. But the feeling self is opened up by the physical experience of touch. When we make room for personal encounter with Jesus through

8. Smith, *You Are What You Love*, 85.

imaginative prayer, we can reconnect with our deeper and often hidden emotions. Morton Kelsey summarizes this dynamic as follows:

> When prayer and meditation concentrate only on concepts they do not touch the most profound part of our being except when it happens accidentally. Conceptual thought does not have the same power [to impact us deeply] as the ability to think in images.[9]

ENCOUNTERING THE GAZE OF JESUS

In the imaginative prayer exercise with the story of Zacchaeus above, we see Zacchaeus move from *watching* Jesus to *meeting* Jesus. Just as Zacchaeus thinks he is a safe distance away, hidden and protected, our posture toward Jesus in prayer can sometimes be like someone who sneaks in the back of church, ready at any moment for a quick getaway. But as Jesus approaches Zacchaeus, he stops, looks up, and focuses his gaze on Zacchaeus. In this captivating and profound moment, Jesus singles Zacchaeus out of the crowd and has a one-on-one conversation with him. Though we may begin this story as Zacchaeus, high up the branches of the sycamore tree, safely watching and observing Jesus from a distance, we are immediately drawn into the action when Jesus turns and looks directly at us, the ones hiding here in this imagined tree. This moment of personal, intimate recognition can come as a shock and surprise, especially if we are not expecting it.

For many years, one of my friends was unable to look directly in people's eyes. She had grown up quite shy, with a strong sense of her own unworthiness. Though she had been a Christian for over forty years she had never experienced Jesus looking directly at her in prayer. When she encountered his loving gaze in this story she was deeply moved. Shortly after this exercise she began to notice her ability, quite unconsciously at first, to look at people more directly in her interactions with them. She attributed this shift to the profoundly healing experience of being seen and noticed by Jesus in prayer. Once she felt *seen* by Jesus, she experienced a new kind of freedom in her life and relationships as well as a deep sense of being known and loved by God.

In another imaginative prayer exercise, I invited people to imagine themselves attending a dinner party as a friend of Jesus. One man said that when he and Jesus got up to leave and thank the hosts, Jesus gave him a little smile and then winked at him. "It was like the entire universe swallowed my

9. Kelsey, *The Other Side of Silence*, 178.

heart," he told me. A week later, that wink was still with him. "It has opened up all kinds of things for me," he said, "acceptance by Jesus, love, friendship, fun. He *wants* me." Interestingly, I have heard many people speak of Jesus winking at them, and it always moves them in profound ways. The wink symbolizes a beautifully personal sense of being *seen* in prayer. Many of us struggle to believe that God notices us or even knows who we are. The wink says, "I see you. I know you. I care about you."

Sometimes when Jesus looks at us, his gaze lovingly convicts us of sin—we realize all the ways we have been looking elsewhere for life and satisfaction. Like a guilty child who finds it difficult to look her mother in the eye, we avoid Jesus' gaze if we sense that our sin will be exposed. Remember the devastating look that Jesus gives Peter after the rooster crows during Jesus' trial? As Luke says, "The Lord turned and looked straight at Peter" (22:61). While this look is not a comforting look, it is loving and healing because it helps Peter remember who he is to Jesus—and who Jesus is to him. Though Peter is afraid and denies Jesus, this look draws his attention back to Jesus. After this look, Peter remembers the word the Lord spoke to him: "Before the rooster crows today, you will disown me three times." Then Luke tells us that Peter "went outside and wept bitterly" (Luke 22:61–62). The immediate pain of this look must have been overwhelming for Peter, but ultimately it is a gift for him.

Several years ago, a group of child psychologists created the "Still Face" experiment,[10] in order to study the impact that a mother's engaged attention has on a young infant. In the experiment, the researcher has a mother sit directly in front of her several-month-old infant who is facing her in a highchair. The mother looks directly at the infant in an animated way, smiling, making loving sounds, keeping the infant's gaze. The child is happy and playful. The mother then turns away from the child, forms an expressionless and unmovable face, and then turns back toward her child, remaining still for several minutes. The child expects the same connection as before but quickly realizes that her mother is not responding. The child becomes increasingly agitated to the point of squealing and crying until the mother, mercifully, reanimates and connects again with her child. The video is difficult to watch, as you witness the extreme discomfort of the child when the mother fails to respond.

10. You can see it on YouTube at UMass Chan Medical School Psychiatry Dept, "The 'Still Face' Experiment."

When I first watched this experiment, I resonated deeply with the baby's experience. I had felt this expressionless, "still" face from God for years. God did not seem to see me or interact with me in any meaningful way. I felt as if I had been squirming and squealing like the distressed infant for most of my Christian life. There was no real God there, just a cardboard cutout God. But over time, Jesus began to turn and look at me in prayer—sometimes with the most exquisite look of warmth and welcome, sometimes with conviction, but always with a loving invitation to return home to him.

When Jesus notices us and looks at us in prayer, we experience the mystery of both his full humanity and his full divinity. It is not particularly meaningful or powerful to imagine someone looking at us, since people look at us all the time, even in our dreams and other imaginative experiences. But when Jesus looks at us—the one whom we worship as our Saviour, the one who created us and sustains our lives—when *he* looks at us, it pierces our heart, and we know we are loved with an everlasting love.

A REAL JESUS

When we prayerfully imagine ourselves in the stories of Jesus, we are interacting with a human being, not a disembodied spirit. Jesus walked the earth as a man, and so we can interact with him as a person. As Richard Foster says, "You can *actually* encounter the living Christ in the event, be addressed by His voice and be touched by His healing power. It can be more than an exercise of the imagination; it can be a genuine confrontation. Jesus Christ will actually come to you."[11] By coming to us, Jesus is drawing us deeper into relationship with him. Philip Sheldrake describes the experience this way: "The imagined scene is only a means. The end is some kind of personal encounter with the Lord which touches the deepest parts of my reality."[12]

This encounter draws us in, asking for a response. As the encounter with Jesus becomes more personal, we are invited to respond, just as we would in any real-life relationship. We cannot simply interact with God as an idea or a static object without some response on our part. If Jesus is only an idea or a philosophy, then I can listen, accept or reject, ponder, ruminate, or discard at will. There is no demand upon me. I am in control.

11. Foster, *Prayer*, 26.
12. Sheldrake, "Imagination and Prayer," 93.

A personal encounter, however, requires more of me. This is also true in our other relationships as well. It is far easier to disregard emails or text requests from people than it is to ignore or refuse them when they are standing right in front of us. Encounter demands response. The process of imaginative prayer moves us from meditation (our own internal thinking and reflecting) to contemplation (listening and interaction with a real "other."). This movement invites us to *listen* and then *respond*.

In the next chapter, we will explore our response as we begin to follow Jesus.

IMAGINATIVE PRAYER EXERCISE: THE TEACHER AND THE FISH (LUKE 5:1–11)

You are a fisherman. It has been a long night of fishing but you've come in with nothing. You're tired and sullen. As you approach the shore, through the early morning fog, you see a crowd gathering by the water's edge so you suggest to the others in the boat that you move down the beach a little so you will have room to wash the nets.

As you clean the nets, you look around. What do you notice about the sky? the lake? the other boats? Is the air still, or can you feel a breeze?

You look at the crowd forming on the beach around a man who seems to be teaching them. People continue to flock onto the beach from the surrounding hills. As you watch the crowd grow, the teacher moves closer to your boat.

What do you feel as you watch this crowd? What are you thinking as this man gets closer to you and your friends?

You look around to make sure you can see all your tools and equipment.

You can't hear what the man is saying, but you think you recognize him from town.

You look back to the nets. This washing will be finished soon, and then you can get some sleep.

Then, you hear your name. You look up, and the man is asking if he can get into your boat so that the people can hear him.

How do you respond? Do you hesitate? Do you feel honored?

You exchange a look with your friends and decide to take the teacher on board, but you hope this will not take too long. You are dead tired.

"Can we push off a little from shore?" he asks. "The people will be able to hear better."

You push off slightly. The boat rocks in the water. You continue to clean your nets as the teacher speaks. Something in his voice captures your attention—it is strong, but gentle. You put down the nets and listen more closely to his teaching. He is speaking about his Father, of the Kingdom of God.

After a few minutes, the teacher dismisses the crowd. As people begin to walk away, he turns to you and says, "Put out into deep water and let down your nets for a catch."

"Master," you stutter, "We have been out all night and caught nothing."

He looks at you, waiting, but saying nothing.

"Because you say so," you say, "I will let down the nets."

You set out in the boat, and the teacher comes along for the ride. What are you thinking as you row out into the lake? You have heard stories of this man named Jesus. After rowing for several minutes, you come to deeper water. What are you thinking as you and the others gather up your clean nets and toss them over the side?

You feel exhausted. You have done this all night, right in this spot.

Then the boat jostles, and the nets suddenly pull against the side of the boat, which begins to list heavily to one side. You call out to your friends to help as you see the nets bulging with fish, straining with the great weight. You work furiously to bring in all the fish, filling both boats until you're afraid you might not make it back to shore.

When you finally reach the shore, you begin unloading the fish. After a while, you look up at Jesus. He looks steadily back at you—through you.

What do you feel as you meet his gaze?

Suddenly, everything that you have ever done wrong suddenly floods your mind—all the times you have been angry and shouted your contempt at others, all the greed and envy that has overtaken you. Who is this man who makes you feel all of this?

You fall at his feet, holding your head and turning away from him.

"Go away from me, Lord. I am sinful."

You wait and listen, but you only hear the water lapping the shore. You wait for Jesus to walk away.

Silence.

Then you feel a hand on the top of your head. "Do not be afraid," Jesus says. "From now on you will catch men rather than fish."

How do you feel as you hear Jesus' words? What do you notice about Jesus' hand? What do you notice about yourself? What do you want to say to Jesus?

CHAPTER 6

Following Jesus

"My sheep listen to my voice;
I know them and they follow me."

—John 10:27

ALL OF US HAVE experience meeting new people. For some of us it's a joy and adventure, for others it's far more fear-inducing and intimidating. Whatever your experience is with meeting new people you know intuitively how to engage with them. After you get past asking their name and where they are from, you might ask them what they do for a living or what kind of hobbies they enjoy. If they are interesting and enjoyable you might be a little bolder and ask them to join you for a coffee or lunch so you can learn more about them. When I first met Rob I was a rookie tree planter in the middle of nowhere in northern British Columbia. I barely knew what I was doing and felt awkward and alone. The only person I knew on the crew was the cook so when Rob invited me to share a tent with him I was relieved. Soon, as we lay there exhausted each night trying to go to sleep, Rob began opening up all kinds of things about his life, his family, his friends, his faith. He had this uncanny ability to make me feel cared for even though he hardly knew me. It wasn't long before Rob became a very close and dear friend.

When Jesus first met people he would often invite them to follow him. This is probably not the way your conversation goes when you first meet someone. But what Jesus meant by that invitation was not too far off what we mean when we invite our new friend for lunch. We usually use the phrase "following Jesus" metaphorically, to mean *believing* in him but Jesus uses this phrase much more literally to invite people to get up, put one foot in front of the other, and physically follow him—to go where he is going. He invites people to be with him, to listen to his teaching, to pay attention to the way he lives and loves, and to follow him on his journey. As Eugene Peterson says, "Following Jesus doesn't get us where we want to go. It gets us where Jesus goes."[1] Jesus wants his friends to follow him so they can get to know him intimately and, eventually, take on his way of life as their own. In the same way, he invites *us* to follow him so that we can forge a friendship with him, listening to each other and sharing our lives together so we, too, might be shaped by his life.

GETTING TO KNOW JESUS

With our friends and acquaintances, we don't talk about "following" to describe the early phase of a relationship. Rather, we use words such as "interested," "attracted," or "intrigued." We want to spend time with our friends to get to know them, discover what makes them tick, what they care about, what kind of person they are. When we first meet someone, we typically exchange preliminary information about ourselves—our names, where we live, what kind of work we do. But as we spend time together, we begin to reveal more of who we are to one another—things we love, things we fear, dreams for the future. As we spend time together and share experiences, we slowly begin to share our hearts with one another. These are the common dynamics of the early stages of any relationship.

What do these early stages of a friendship look like with Jesus? What does it look like to "spend time" with Jesus? Many of us might think of going to church, spending time with other Christians, talking about spiritual things, or reading our Bibles. These are all good things to do but they can still feel overly cognitive and detached from Jesus as a person. What if "spending time" with Jesus could look a little more like it does in our other relationships?

Though we do not hear about many early *conversations* between Jesus and his disciples in the Gospels, we do see the early stages of their relationship. They learn one another's names, spend time together and share experiences. John tells us that Andrew, Peter's brother, and another

1. Peterson, *Jesus Way*, 242.

friend "spent the day with [Jesus]" after they first met him (John 1:39). The disciples accompany Jesus to a wedding feast (John 2:1–11) and Jesus spends time at their homes (Luke 5:29). Throughout the Gospels, we see the disciples accompanying Jesus as he travels from town to town, teaching and performing miracles. Many of these journeys would have taken several days. During that time, their relationship would have been slowly taking shape as they talked together, laughed together, learned together, and lived their daily life together.

During those early days, the disciples are not doing very much as they begin to follow Jesus. In fact, after the initial calling of the disciples in the early pages of the Gospels, they seem to disappear altogether for several chapters. They are present, but Jesus does not seem to have any expectations of them. He simply asks them to "come," and they do. He does not seem concerned with what they believe or with getting things right. Apparently, he just wants them to be *with him*.

I wish I had noticed this when I was young and wrestling with what it meant to "follow Jesus," which I understood as giving my whole life to him all at once. Growing up in a context where you hear weekly invitations to "give your life to Jesus" can create the impression that the first step is the *only* step. Once you decide to "follow Jesus" you are fully committed. Yet no other relationship works like this! Trust and commitment need time to develop. Jesus knows this. The disciples themselves do not fully give their lives to Jesus until the later chapters of the Gospels—if not the early chapters of Acts. Moreover, Jesus does not even ask the disciples to give their lives to him when he first meets them. He simply says, "Follow me."

Throughout those early days together, Jesus gives space and time for his relationships with the disciples to take root and grow. As they spend time together, Jesus nurtures their trust over the course of many weeks and months. This time is essential for the development of real friendships.

When we respond to Jesus' call to "follow me," we, too, are invited to get to know him slowly. We might do this as we read about him in the Gospels and spend time with others who are also following him. We may listen to sermons, take Bible courses, and become involved in-service projects and worship services. But prayer is the primary place where we get to know Jesus and spend time with him. Imaginative prayer opens up this experience for us, inviting us to join his first friends as they accompany Jesus on his journey and get to know him over time. As we notice the way he interacts with people and listen in on his conversations, we get a window into his heart of love and compassion. We find ourselves attracted to him, wanting to know more about him, wanting him to know more about us. We see, in "real time," the love he has for Mary and Martha as he responds to their questions and their grief. We feel the deep desire to be touched and healed by Jesus as we place ourselves in the role of the blind man seeking healing. Imaginative prayer invites us to *be* these people and respond to Jesus' invitation to friendship. Like any new relationship, the more time we spend with Jesus, the more our interest in and attraction for him grows.

IMAGINATIVE PRAYER EXERCISE: COME AND SEE (JOHN 1:35–39)

We are sitting, you and I, on a small patch of grass next to a noisy marketplace. We have been walking for quite a while with our rabbi, John (whom many people call "The Baptizer"). We are tired and thirsty, so we have stopped to enjoy some shade and water. We are asking John about what happened yesterday, down at the river. We haven't stopped thinking about the man who asked to be baptized—how uncomfortable he seemed to make our rabbi and how terrified we were when the heavens opened. Neither of us slept all night because we couldn't stop thinking about the day. Now our rabbi is saying such incredible things about this Jesus—how he will baptize with the Holy Spirit, and how he is the Son of God, the promised One for our people. As we listen to him, we feel like we are being swept into this powerful hope, something that is somehow *choosing* us.

Our whole lives have been nothing but fishing—all those hours on the water, waiting, hauling, cleaning, selling. But listening to our rabbi talk about this Jesus as the promised Messiah, it's like something is beckoning us to go find him and go wherever he goes. We have never given any thought to anything but fishing and yet we feel this strong urge to get up and go looking for this Jesus. The more John talks about Jesus, the stronger the desire grows to know more about this man, to hear what he has to say. We want to meet him, listen to him, find out who he is.

As John begins to respond to our hurried questions, he pauses and looks up, focusing on the road beyond us. Then his eyes widen and he smiles broadly, pointing.

"Look," he says, "the Lamb of God."

We follow his pointing finger and see the man from the river—Jesus! Jumping to our feet we hurry toward him as he walks calmly along the road, our hearts pounding. We pause as we get close to him, not sure what we're actually doing. What will we say? What will *he* say? We whisper to each other as we approach him.

Suddenly, Jesus stops and looks at us.

"What do you want?" he asks.

What do we *want*?

"Uh," we both stutter, "Where are you staying, Rabbi?"

He smiles. "Why don't you come and see?"

So we go and see where he is staying and spend that day with him

~

Pause and imagine Jesus looking directly at you and asking, "What do you want?" Give this question time to sink slowly into your heart.

What do I want?

What responses fill your mind? Try not to edit them. If you do not know how to respond, invite the Spirit to help you reflect on this question: *What do I want from Jesus?*

Take a few minutes to reflect on what it would be like to spend the day with Jesus. Having just met him, what would you ask him? What would you tell him about yourself?

Now imagine Jesus inviting you to "come and see" where he is staying. What might it look like for you to "come and see" Jesus at this point in your journey? What do you imagine about the place where he is staying? What are you feeling as you spend time with him?

TAKING ROOT

Think about someone you now consider to be a good friend. What initially attracted you to this person? What was especially interesting about her or his story? As your friendship has developed over time, what has kept you intrigued?

Now think about your relationship with Jesus. Do you find yourself attracted to him as a person? Does your relationship continue to be dynamic and alive, as it is with other friendships? What is it like to talk to him? To listen to him?

Some years ago, a good friend of mine went to see a spiritual director to talk about her struggle with God. After listening to her story, the director offered her some simple advice; stop praying. It was shocking advice but it was important to see if she missed God, to see if her affections for God would be stirred through the absence. Her spiritual life had become a series of obligations and theological entanglements, and she needed to fall in love with the person of Jesus again, to go back to the root of their relationship and discover what was there.

Many of us use the language of having "a relationship with Jesus" quite freely. For many believers, having "a relationship with Jesus" is simply another way to say "Christian." But if we think about this more honestly we might recognize that this language does not describe the actual nature of what is happening between ourselves and Jesus. If you struggle, as I did for years, to know whether or not you have actually *met* Jesus, then *following*, or *relating* to him will be even more confusing. For a long time, my *relationship* with God was like a treasure chest that promised gold and jewels beyond imagining, but when I opened it, it was completely empty. Having a "relationship with God" sounded so good, so rich and meaningful, but if I was honest with myself, when I opened the "relationship" lid, there was nothing there.

Many years ago, I had a brief conversation with a woman who said, "You Christians say you have a relationship with Jesus, but how do you have a relationship with a dead guy?" How indeed! Her question haunted me for weeks. What difference did it make to me that Jesus was alive and wanted to relate to me personally? The gospel I believed—that Jesus had died for the forgiveness of my sins and that I was now righteous before the Father—did not seem to require a *living* Jesus. What did Jesus' *alive-ness* mean in my life? And how could I relate to him? I knew the theology but did I *know* this Jesus? Could I really say that I had a living, active *relationship* with him? If I was completely honest, Jesus was more like a casual acquaintance—someone who had saved me (so I was told) but with whom I struggled to relate on a day-to-day basis. What I had with God fell far short of a relationship—and further still from friendship, a word Jesus himself uses to describe the nature of the relationship he is inviting us to develop with him. In spite of all my years of being a follower of Jesus, I had formed a theoretical construct rather than a living relationship.

Yet the metaphorical language throughout the biblical narrative suggests that we can relate to God in a deeply personal and intimate way. We are sheep who know the shepherd's voice (John 10:10). We are the bride and he is the Bridegroom (Song of Songs). We are his children and he is our Father (Luke 15). Paul says often that because we are in Christ, we are invited to participate in the life of God himself. This metaphorical language evokes a reality that is difficult to comprehend even while it stirs our longings to love and be loved by God personally. How can the God of the universe possibly offer us this degree of relational intimacy?

When we watch Jesus interacting with people in the Gospels, we see an intimately personal God in action. As Jesus forms friendships and cares for people, he reveals the very nature and character of God. God is giving and receiving love constantly within Godself. This three-in-one God *is* relationship. Aelred of Rievaulx, the twelfth-century monk and author, goes so far as to say, "God is friendship . . . He who dwells in friendship dwells in God"[2] We might add, he who dwells in God dwells in friendship. Forming and nurturing friendships is who God is and what God does.

But relating to God can be a complicated thing, for God is not like us. How do we relate to God personally? In our human relationships, we use our bodies and senses to experience other people and form living relationships with them. Relationships require bodies, and God does not have a body. Yet Jesus *does* have a body, and the disciples related to him in bodily form. It might seem that they had a decided advantage over us because they could listen to his words and tone of voice, watch his gestures and expressions as he spoke to them. Because they could pick up all the non-verbal communication, they could see the love in his eyes, the warmth of his embrace, the joy of his physical presence.

But quite mysteriously, Jesus tells his disciples, "It is for your good that I am going away. Unless I go the Counselor will not come to you." (John 16:7). Even though his body will soon depart from them, he will be with them in a whole new way, a better way, because the Spirit will come to live within them. The physical departure of Jesus opens up the possibility of a deeper intimacy, moving from him being *with* us to being *in* us.

Then Jesus says a rather curious thing. "Before long the world will not see me anymore, but you will see me" (John 14:19). While he might have been speaking about his resurrection appearances, he also might have been referring to a new way that his friends would be able to *see* him even though he would no longer be visible in bodily form. Perhaps he was promising them the kind of sight that Elisha prayed for his servant boy to receive—a sight that comes from the indwelling Spirit. With this new vision, the

---

2. Aelred of Rievaulx, *Spiritual Friendship*, 18.

disciples would mysteriously be able to know and experience Jesus' presence with them through the presence of the Spirit dwelling within them.

These first disciples had seen Jesus in the flesh, but now they would know the ongoing presence of Jesus through the Spirit. We, too, have the presence of this same Spirit living within us, who brings us an awareness of Jesus' presence. Imaginative prayer offers us a taste of this encounter with the physical Jesus as we see him walking, talking, and interacting with people. Then, when he turns to us and invites us into friendship, we can engage with him as we might engage in any relationship, spending time together, sharing our hearts and listening to him.

TALKING TOGETHER

One essential aspect of any growing relationship is communication—how we reveal who we are to our friends as well as tell our stories and share our hearts. Throughout Scripture, beginning with Adam and Eve, God reveals himself through language, talking to people and inviting them to respond through prayer.[3] In the Gospels, as we see Jesus, listen to his words, and bring our longings and desires to him, we often discover that Jesus will speak personally to us. He does not simply point to a passage of Scripture, nor refer us to a conversation he had with someone else, but engages us personally, similar to conversations we have with other friends.

While this may sound strange—or even scandalous—we can't really have a personal relationship with someone if we never converse. Jesus wants to talk with us about our personal struggles, the sins we are battling, the doubts we are nursing, so that he can bring his love, care, and attention into the details of our daily lives. Conversations with Jesus are, of course, different than conversations we have with others in our life. Sometimes they can be quite direct and clear, other times they can seem more like sensing than hearing. When we do experience God speaking to us, it is wise to share this with a friend or spiritual director, who can help us discern what is from the Lord and what might be our own thoughts and unconscious projections. It is rarely black and white. Of course, anything we hear from Jesus must always align with Scripture.

---

3. There are many good books that speak about this conversational dynamic. See Dallas Willard, *Hearing God: Developing a Conversational Relationship with God* and Adam S. McHugh, *The Listening Life*.

Our conversation with Jesus through imaginative prayer can help us come to know Jesus as a real person, who lived a human life, enjoyed common events, and behaved in ordinary ways. One woman described her experience imagining herself at the wedding with Jesus in the town of Cana (Jn 2:1–11). "I'm a guest at the wedding," she writes, "and Jesus is talking to me, just telling stories about his family, and growing up in Nazareth and other places. I feel included, drawn in, feeling like I belong to Jesus." She felt that she could actually get to know this Jesus as a person rather than an abstraction. We form relationships with people by talking to them, listening to them, learning who they are and what they love. The same is true in our relationship with Jesus. Many people struggle to relate to Jesus precisely because they do not experience Jesus as a real person. They feel they are supposed to relate to him and follow him, but they have little experience actually interacting with him.

Ronald Rolheiser argues that our inability to experience Jesus as a real person has led to our modern age of unbelief. He writes,

> God is not experienced as a living person to whom we actually talk, person to person, and from whom we seek final consolation and comfort . . . rather, God is experienced and related to as a religion, a church, a moral philosophy, a guide for private virtue.[4]

Jesus has become, for many of us, more like an idea than a real person. But no relationship can be forced—with God or with people. Any relationship with God is a gift rather than an achievement. We must wait in expectant anticipation to receive whatever is given. While some people say they have never heard God speak to them apart from the Bible, others can recount lengthy and profound conversations with the Lord. This is a mystery. Though God seems to operate differently with different people, he invites all of us to come to him honestly with our longings for connection and relationship.

FORMING A REAL RELATIONSHIP

Imaginative prayer enables us to experience a real relationship with Jesus as we enter into his life as it is portrayed in the Gospels. Morton Kelsey describes this experience as follows:

4. Rolheiser, *Shattered Lantern*, 16.

When one lives with Christ in these various experiences, Jesus becomes as real as the people with whom one sits down to eat dinner at night, or even more real. He becomes a person to whom one can turn and speak in the hours of quiet late at night or early in the morning. He becomes a friend who waits with open arms on the other side of silence.[5]

But how can we relate to Jesus in this way? It may seem ludicrous to reduce the grandeur of God to a dinner guest. If this is your reaction, try to hold it loosely, since our reactions often come from places of inexperience and uneasiness. While you may be unaccustomed to encountering the human intimacy and reality of Jesus, do you find that you long for just such a relationship? Are you longing to have conversations with Jesus? Are you longing to relate to Jesus more intimately?

When we enter into Gospel stories in prayer, we are invited to encounter Jesus in everyday life, his and ours, and begin to share ourselves more and more openly. It becomes a truly human experience as we interact with the humanity of Jesus.

Many Christians tend to emphasize the divinity of Jesus over his humanity. Because Jesus is our Savior and we worship him, his divinity often takes center stage. We believe that Jesus is fully human and fully divine but can struggle to relate to his humanity. Because we believe that Jesus was more than a wise teacher or spiritual guru, we want to protect his divinity from those who might deny it. The central scandal and tension of Christianity, though, is that Jesus was both a man *and* God incarnate. If Jesus came to us as a man in order to meet us in *our* humanity, what might it look like to engage with him relationally in *his* humanity?

Imaginative prayer can help us engage more fully with the humanity of Jesus. Though praying with Jesus is a mental exercise, it connects us with the bodily humanity of Jesus. As Joseph Whelan writes, "To be 'with' [Jesus] in Gospel stories is to engage with his materiality, his true humanness, which is about the redemption not only of our 'souls' but also of our bodies."[6] In imaginative prayer we walk and interact with Jesus *materially*, rather than merely thinking *thoughts* about him. Our bodies and our emotions can be fully engaged in our encounters with Jesus and, therefore, can also be transformed by Jesus. One friend told me that as she engaged her imagination in prayer, she began to experience Jesus as "in the room" with

5. Kelsey, *The Other Side of Silence*, 213–14.
6. Whelan, "Contemplating Christ," 196.

her rather than simply slipping notes under the door. That evocative image resonated for me, as I had felt for many years that I only had access to Jesus' notes. When we engage with Jesus' humanity, the door swings open wide and our relationship with him will grow and develop as we live alongside him and follow him into deeper and stronger friendship.

IMAGINATIVE PRAYER EXERCISE. CALLING MATTHEW (LUKE 5:27-32)

You are at your booth dealing with the tax payments from a long line of people. You accept their payments and record the amount on one of the official documents piled on your table. Many of the townspeople mutter snide comments as they pass by your booth, but you are used to their contempt by now. Over time, you have learned to ignore them. No one really knows you anyway. No one has ever asked what brought you to this place, this job.

The sun is beginning to set and the last person in line steps away, finished with their transaction. You busily pack up the piles of papers scattered across the table. Some have fallen to the ground. As you bend to pick them up you hear approaching footsteps. *Go away*, you say to yourself. The footsteps stop, and you sense someone standing in front of your table. You look up reluctantly. It is the miracle-worker you've seen around town. Several other men also approach, gathering around your table. You recognize them as companions of the Stranger. Your body tenses up as you take a step back. You wonder what they want from you.

Jesus looks at you directly, then says, "Matthew."

You are surprised he knows your name.

"Matthew," he says again, "I want you to follow me."

As you look at Jesus looking at you, how do you feel as you ponder this invitation? What do you notice about him and his followers? What questions do you want to ask Jesus? Take a few minutes to reflect on how you want to respond to this invitation.

∾

The following day you busily invite all your friends to come to dinner at your house so they can meet this Jesus who has captured your heart. You hardly know what it means to "follow him" but you have chosen to do so, whatever it might entail.

Sitting at the table you look around the room. Musicians have set up in the corner and are playing for the guests. People are talking and laughing. Listen to the music. Breathe it all in.

You notice people as you have never noticed them before. You see your friends leaning in and listening to Jesus, asking him questions, amazed at his answers.

What do you notice about Jesus? How do you feel as you watch your friends, including Jesus, enjoying this banquet?

Suddenly, you overhear a group of pastors at a table behind you, muttering loudly, harshly accusing some of Jesus' disciples for eating with tax collectors and prostitutes.

Their words burn. You feel your face flush as the room falls into an awkward silence.

Then Jesus stands up and faces the pastors. "It is not the healthy that need a doctor but the sick. I have not come to call the righteous but sinners to repentance."

What does Jesus look like as he says this? What do you hear in his tone of voice? As you remain in the scene, how do you want to respond to Jesus?

CHAPTER 7

Trusting Jesus

Overhearing what they said, Jesus told him,
"Don't be afraid; just believe."

—Mark 5:36

IT MAY SEEM ODD to make a distinction between "following Jesus" and "trusting Jesus," as these two ideas are usually combined when we think about our spiritual lives. To follow Jesus *means* to trust him. But considered in the light of a developing relationship, we can see that following Jesus might look more like taking tentative steps to get to know him, whereas trusting him involves a deeper commitment that emerges gradually over time. If someone we recently met asks to borrow our brand-new car or offers to look after our kids for a weekend, we would probably hesitate. Wisdom tells us to wait until we know them better. Trust within relationships takes time. It does not happen immediately. Trust is like a slow growing tree. When first planted, it is fragile and needs lots of care and attention. As it grows it strengthens; it is able to sustain high winds and eventually offer shade from a scorching sun. When we first meet Jesus and decide to start following him, our trust is like a tender sapling. As we turn toward him and listen more and more to what he has to say, our trust in him begins to sprout, but it will not develop deep roots until we have followed him for many miles.

I first met Jeff when we were in high school. Our brothers were best friends and they thought we should meet—perhaps we would become close friends as well. It did not happen then—much to our brothers' disappointment, I think—but a few years later, when we found ourselves living in the same city, we began taking tentative steps of friendship toward each other. Trust slowly began to grow. It soon flourished. Jeff asked me for advice about something. I went to him with a pernicious struggle in my life. He slowly opened his life to me, trusting me with the deep things of his heart and inviting me to do the same. We discovered we could share our pain and name our longings to each other and they would be held and honored. Tears would flow often in our conversations. Jeff relentlessly called me back to Jesus by his patient listening. He became a model of Jesus' friendship to me. Trust has solidified in our friendship to the point where it is difficult to imagine trusting him more than I already do. Strong friendships take time to grow.

Take a moment to think of *your* close friend. One of the things that makes this person close is that you trust them deeply. Can you point to the actual moment when this trust first began? Or has your trust grown over time? For most of us, the more time we spend with someone, the more we reveal ourselves to one another, and as we take risks and share greater depths of our heart, the more trust will deepen and grow. As we deepen our trust with someone, we begin to share our struggles, failures, weaknesses, and shame. With our closest friends, we can become more vulnerable and open about the hidden things in our life because we feel safe and do not need to protect our heart from accusation or rejection. Over time we begin to rely on our close friends for companionship and support, love, and encouragement. If a close friend asks to borrow our car or offers to look after our kids, we will not hesitate for a moment because we trust that friend completely.

Many of us, though, have not been shown that a relationship with Jesus also requires time for trust to develop. We can live under the weight of thinking that Jesus demands our complete trust from the beginning of the relationship. When we are hesitant about trusting Jesus, we feel guilty because we think we *should* trust him. He is the Son of God, after all! But just as with any relationship, we need to get to know Jesus and spend time with him before we can trust him. Even if many people in your life tell you that Jesus is trustworthy, you have to get to know him yourself before you can trust him with the precious things in your life. It might be an immense act of courage and honesty to tell Jesus that you actually do not trust him very much—and need help to do so.

NURTURING TRUST THROUGH PRAYER

How do we allow trust to grow in our relationship with Jesus? Our desire to relate to Jesus, become closer to him, and grow in our trust and love for him can seem extremely ethereal and abstract. Imaginative prayer offers us a concrete way to engage our desire and nurture a relationship of trust with Jesus. When we prayerfully imagine ourselves entering Gospel stories, living with Jesus, listening to him as the disciples did, and noticing how our heart responds, we make space for God to plant the seed of a slow growing "trust" tree within us. When we experience the tenderness, the loving presence, and the care of Jesus over time, we will become more open and vulnerable with him in prayer, trusting him with our struggles, shame, raw emotions, and weaknesses.

Early in my imaginative prayer journey, I was part of a small group who would pray with several Gospel stories throughout the week using our imagination. When we got together we would share our experiences in prayer.[1] After the first few weeks I noticed in my prayers I was always on the outskirts of the crowd that was listening to Jesus in any given scene. I was present and paying attention but at a distance, with folded arms, in a self-protective stance. As soon as I noticed this I recognized how true this was as a visual depiction of my inner posture toward Jesus. I was paying attention to him, "following" him (one might say), but at a safe distance. I was unsure if I could trust him.

Slowly during that season of my life I began to feel a faint but growing desire to be closer to Jesus and to trust him more deeply. I no longer wanted to remain at a distance but I did not know *how* to get closer to Jesus. I knew I could not simply flip a switch and trust more. As I lingered with yet another crowd scene in prayer, I suddenly knew what to do. Though I was unable to flip a "trust-switch," I *could* get my body closer to Jesus in my prayer, symbolizing my desire to be nearer to him and to trust him more. And so, in my imagination, I got up and moved through the crowd toward Jesus. I felt both nervous and excited as my heart began to pound. I plopped myself down directly in front of him. Jesus looked at me and smiled. I felt he was validating my longing to be near him, to love him, to trust him. I still did not know what this "trusting" would look like in my daily life but through my imagination, I was able to express my desire to say "Yes" to Jesus in a tangible way.

1. We were doing the 19th Annotation of the Ignatian *Spiritual Exercises*.

JESUS WAITS FOR TRUST

Jesus honors our need for trust to grow slowly and develop over time in our relationship with him. In Mark 8:27–30, Jesus is walking along the road with his disciples, when he turns and asks them, "Who do people say I am?" After a few options are offered—John the Baptist, Elijah, one of the prophets—Jesus asks, "What about you? Who do you say I am?" We might imagine a pregnant pause as the disciples look at each other and then back at Jesus. After a moment, Peter pipes up and says, "You are the Messiah." This amazing declaration by Peter identifies Jesus as the Messiah of Israel, the one sent by God for their deliverance. At this climactic moment, Peter makes it abundantly clear that he trusts Jesus with his life.

But this is not the first conversation Jesus has with Peter. For months, Jesus has been building a relationship with his disciples. First, he calls them to follow him (Mark 1:14–20). Next, he appoints them as Apostles (Mark 3:13–19). Then he proceeds to teach them about the kingdom of God while journeying with them from town to town, performing many miracles. Throughout the first eight chapters of Mark, the disciples spend time with Jesus, asking their questions, getting things wrong, and expressing both fear and amazement. As mentioned earlier, they do not *do* much at all. They simply watch, listen, and learn.

We do not know how long these early chapters of Mark represent in real time—probably many months, if not a year or more. Throughout this time, the disciples are getting to know Jesus and slowly coming to trust him. After countless hours of conversation and shared experience, he asks them, "Who do you say that I am?" He does not ask them this question when he first meets them. He knows that they have no idea who he is at that point. But after many months, slowly coming to know and trust him, Jesus feels they are ready to answer this question. Jesus knows that he is headed for the cross and he wants to make sure that his friends trust him enough to follow him. As soon as Peter makes this declaration about Jesus' identity, Jesus begins to speak to them about his impending death. He waits for their trust before inviting them to follow him into the next stage of their relationship—when they will have to deny themselves, take up their cross, and possibly lose their lives for his sake.

This timing reveals the loving care that Jesus has for his friends—including you and me. He knows the level of relationship we have with him—how much we can hear from him; how much we trust him. Just as he waited with his disciples until they had a solid relational foundation, he will wait with us until we are ready for the next stage of our friendship.

It is not always easy to know how much we trust Jesus. Because we are *supposed* to trust him, we might be tempted to think we trust him more than we actually do (or less than we actually do!). In Matthew 14, when Jesus asks Peter to step out of his boat and onto the surface of the lake, Peter comes face to face with this question, "Do you trust me?" In the following imaginative prayer exercise, we are going to enter this story as a way to engage this question ourselves. You may want to enhance the experience of imaginative prayer by acting out the story with your body. Let your sofa be the boat, gently floating on the lake. Take a few minutes to close your eyes and place yourself in the boat.

IMAGINATIVE PRAYER EXERCISE: ON THE WATER (MATTHEW 14:22–32)

You are in a fishing boat with your friends on the Lake of Galilee. It is dark. The boat bobs gently on the water. You have been fishing all night and are dead tired.

You feel a shudder beneath you as the wind picks up and the surface of the water begins to churn. The waves grow and your boat starts rocking from side to side. You grab the gunwale to steady yourself. Looking up, you see in the distance a storm cloud bearing down upon you as waves start splashing over the side of the boat. This storm came out of nowhere. The darkness engulfs you. Your heart pounds.

Suddenly someone cries, "*It's a ghost,*" and as you strain your eyes, you see what appears to be a human figure walking toward you over the surface of the water.

"*Take courage!*" a voice says. "*It is I. Do not be afraid.*"

You recognize that voice. You can see him standing there, on the water, Jesus, his robe flapping in the wind, a look of peaceful calm on his face.

You summon your courage. "*Lord,*" you call into the darkness, "*if it's you, tell me to come to you on the water.*"

"*Come,*" he says to you.

Pause here and invite the Spirit to help you live in this moment as if you are actually on the boat, hearing Jesus call out to you.

You hesitate. Slowly, you swing one leg over the gunwale and let it dangle there. Pause and let your eyes lead you. Can you see the whitecaps?

Can you feel them grabbing at your feet? Can you still see Jesus? You gently, nervously swing your other leg over the gunwale. As you sit on the edge of the boat, inches from the water, you take a deep breath before shoving off.

What do you do?

What do you feel?

Where is Jesus?

Come.

Remain in this moment and ask yourself how you will respond. Can you trust Jesus? Do you leap into the water? What are you feeling? Fear? Confusion? Courage? Pride?

THE EMOTIONS OF TRUST

When we first meet someone, it is easy to keep our emotions in reserve and engage through rational thought and conversation. As we get to know and trust them, we slowly reveal the deeper regions of our hearts and emotions. Even though this same dynamic is true in our relationship with Jesus, we can often feel stuck in an overly cognitive posture in prayer rather than experiencing the level of emotional vulnerability and intimacy that we long for. We might desire to go deeper with Jesus and trust him more fully and yet feel lost as to how to open ourselves to engage with him emotionally.

When we enter Gospel stories through imaginative prayer, we are ushered into an emotion-filled landscape of relationship. As we respond to what is happening in the story rather than simply thinking about it, our emotions rise to the surface. As you were sitting on the edge of the boat just now in the prayer exercise above, did you need to *allow* yourself to feel anything? That kind of situation would likely be all feeling and not much thinking. Fear, confusion, courage. All of these and more are simply present within you just as they are in real life experiences.

This is the power of the imagination. It holds our emotions. It allows our emotions to express themselves, even if we are not physically experiencing the situation. It is the presence of our emotions that makes these imagined scenes feel real.

In a doctoral ministry dissertation, Kathryn Fitzgerald recounts the story of a young woman who was struggling with tremendous shame because of an abortion she had some years before. As she prayed with the nativity scene in Luke 2, she sensed Mary prompting her to take the baby Jesus in her arms. At first the young woman recoiled. How could she hold

Jesus after what she had done to her own baby? But she sensed Mary insisting, and so she eventually took the baby Jesus into her arms and began to weep softly, then convulsively, releasing all the pain and shame she had been carrying over her own unborn child. Even as a tiny baby, Jesus brought immense comfort and healing to this woman, helping her unleash her emotions through her imagination.[2]

Imaginative prayer opens up space for us to have deep emotional connections that establish trust with Jesus. I have heard people who pray with their imagination report that they often "end up a mess on the floor" or feel "ready to explode" or feel "completely overwhelmed." Some connect so deeply with Jesus that they feel "undone" or "broken open" as tears begin to flow freely. Tears are often a sign that Jesus is reaching the depths of our heart as we experience extremely painful and difficult emotions. We might feel rageful anger, debilitating fear, or intense resistance, but as we experience Jesus caring for us, encouraging our emotional expressions, and loving us through them, trust begins to grow.

Friendships involve both parties opening themselves to one another. This is true in our relationship with Jesus as well. As much as we may desire to open up our emotions with Jesus, when we look at the Gospels, we see Jesus opening himself up first, allowing his disciples to see his heart and experience him as an emotional being. As we interact with Jesus in imaginative prayer, *we* will experience Jesus' emotional life as well.

WITNESSING THE EMOTIONS OF JESUS

In chapter 4, I talked about seeing Jesus full of joy as he laughed and played with children in an imaginative prayer experience. His emotion drew me in, stirring the longing in my heart for a deeper and more real connection with him. George Aschenbrenner, a Jesuit scholar who has written extensively on imaginative prayer, says that "as each contemplation is repeated and passes into another, we are glimpsing more and more clearly the very inner life and heart of God."[3] We not only read about God's love, care, and compassion for people, we also experience it and feel it. When we see Jesus as a real man with feelings and genuinely human responses to life, joy, and pain, this revelation is a revelation of God himself. As the writer of Hebrews tells us, Jesus is the "radiance of God's glory and the exact representation

2. Fitzgerald, "Central Role of Imagination," 44.

3. Aschenbrenner, "Becoming Whom We Contemplate," 35.

of his being" (Hebrews 1:3). Jesus reveals God to us—and Jesus is an emotional being.

Yet when reading the stories in the Gospels, I would often experience Jesus as gliding into a scene, saying or doing something amazing, and then walking away somewhat austere and remote. He did not seem like a real person with real human emotions. It was only when Jesus *did* express emotion—at the tomb of Lazarus or the Garden of Gethsemane, for example—that I would feel a deep affinity and connection with him. It was his raw emotional responses that touched me. I recognized myself in these responses. Emotions work to bind us together.

Jesus was a "man of sorrows," but also filled with the joy of the Lord, and scripture reveals that he also felt anger, elation, disappointment, and grief. These emotions were all evident to those who walked the roads of Palestine with him. When we enter into these scenes with Jesus, we are invited to experience the full range of the emotional life of God.

In Mark 2, some men bring their paralyzed friend to be healed by Jesus, but they find the house crowded and a path to Jesus completely blocked. They decide to rip open the roof and lower their friend down in order to place him directly in front of Jesus. It would have taken a long time for these men to make a hole large enough for a man in that roof. What do you imagine Jesus doing all this time? Is he smiling, trying to ignore all the commotion? One friend who entered this story in prayer writes,

> I imagined the straw-dried mud and dust falling on Jesus' head. I see the commotion on the ceiling, I hear the shouts of the crowd. I see Jesus. I imagine him throwing his head back in laughter as the man is lowered down in front of him, even applauding, as if to say, 'Now *that's* what I'm talkin' about!'

Can you hear the exaltation in Jesus' voice? When we talked about this experience later, my friend said, "I felt the joy of Jesus, it was so invitational—it just filled me up!" The people who witnessed this scene in the house that day did not simply "learn a lesson" from Jesus. They witnessed him loving this man in an extraordinary, self-revelatory way as Jesus responded compassionately and healed him. Jesus was no Stoic philosopher. He lived the "joy of the Lord" within his very Being. My friend received a glimpse of the heart of God through this scene that day, a heart full of love, compassion, and joy.

When we put ourselves into these scenes, we get a real taste of the emotional atmosphere, which we often lose when we become over-familiar with a story from the Gospels. Not all Jesus' emotional responses are positive, of course. Negative emotions are also a part of his life. While we enjoy watching Jesus as he plays and laughs with children, we may struggle to remain present when he is angry or in agony. But these moments were also part of his life, which we are invited to share.

The scene of Jesus angrily clearing the Temple (Mark 11:15–18) is so emotional and explosive that it can be troubling to enter imaginatively. One friend who imagined the vividness describes her experience as follows:

> I look and see Peter and am alarmed by his expression—he is staring at Jesus. He then rushes over to him, calling out. I try to make sense of what I'm seeing—Jesus, it seems, has snapped. He is yelling, pushing over stalls, kicking, upending tables, scattering money. We don't know if we should grab hold of Jesus and get him out before he is arrested. I can't help but wonder if he has some kind of death wish to be acting this way.

The disciples must have wondered what Jesus was doing as they witnessed this chaos, shouting, and cursing. Do you imagine them entering the melee or distancing themselves from Jesus? If you were standing there, would you join in with Jesus or stand back? We often approach these stories by trying to figure out the *point* Jesus was making. While such inquiries are important to understanding Jesus' mission, the disciples were not thinking this way as the tables flew around the temple courtyard. They were caught up in the intensity, seeing a ferocity in Jesus they had not witnessed before. This experience must have informed how they remembered this episode—and remembered Jesus. It may have also reframed how they thought about anger or their own experience of anger. Our theological understanding and emotional growth will be transformed as we experience the human emotions of Jesus.

Another friend was deeply impacted when he imaginatively entered the story of Lazarus in John 11. When the scene opens, Lazarus has already died and been in the tomb for days. As my friend Michael prayerfully entered the scene, he found himself standing by Lazarus' tomb, watching Jesus as he wept with grief. "I watched him cry, wail, scream, kick, pick up a branch and start whacking it against a tree before he finally collapsed," Michael recounted. The NIV says that Jesus was "deeply moved in spirit and troubled" (John 11:33). The Greek word that is translated here as "troubled," *embrimaomai,* means "to roar, storm with anger . . . enraged, grieved, agitated."[4] If we were to see this being lived out, it might resemble what Michael saw as he imagined Jesus grieving the death of his friend. When he first engaged this story imaginatively in prayer, Michael had recently lost a friend in a tragic accident and was struggling to find God in the midst of his grief. Watching Jesus express such anger and pain was deeply healing for Michael because he could tangibly see that Jesus knew real suffering and loss. This helped him trust Jesus with his own pain. Until this experience, Michael had been quite guarded and resistant in prayer because he was so angry at God for allowing his friend to die. As he observed Jesus expressing his grief, Michael felt safe enough to talk to Jesus about his own pain.

When we pay attention to Jesus' emotional responses to situations in the Gospels, he will become more deeply human to us. Rather than remaining distant and detached from a scene, Jesus gets his hands dirty, his eyes well up with tears, his muscles tense, and his body expresses emotion. In all these responses Jesus invites us into a new level of trust.

EXPRESSING OUR EMOTIONS TO JESUS

As we experience Jesus' authentic emotions and feel freer to express our own emotions to him, a relationship of trust will be nurtured between us. Like Jesus, we experience both positive and negative emotions, but we often struggle to reveal our negative emotions in prayer. We are ashamed of feeling fearful, angry, or frustrated, so we don't want to talk about these emotions with Jesus. Yet honestly expressing our emotions builds intimacy in all of our relationships. If we only allow ourselves to feel positive emotions, we are likely hiding, avoiding, or burying our negative feelings, which leaves an important part of ourselves hidden. We can only grow and mature in our relationships when we have the courage to express the full range of our emotional life. Through imaginative prayer, we expose our emotional life to God and invite him to bring healing into our darker places. Our emotions are integral to our imaginative prayer experiences.

Throughout the Gospels, Jesus tells his friends not to be afraid. This suggests that his presence and actions often evoked fear in people. But we tend to ignore our fear of Jesus, thinking of him as perpetually loving and inviting. One woman describes how she discovered the fear of Jesus in her own heart during prayer one day.

4. See Zodhiates, "embromaomai," 574.

> I feel very connected to the fear the disciples felt as they entered the cloud (on the Mount of Transfiguration). I feel afraid, too. I feel afraid that if I join Jesus he will ask me to do something I don't want to do. And even worse, he would ask me to do it and then forget about me.

After making this discovery, this woman shared some of the deeper fears that she harbored in her life with Jesus and discussed them intentionally in her prayer life with God. The imagined scene helped her to connect with this and process it more intentionally with God.

Some of us may have been raised to believe that it is not proper to express negative emotions to God. We may have been taught that expressing our anger or frustration is dishonoring or disobedient to God. When we learn this as children, we may find it difficult to express our real emotions to God as adults. When I was leading a prayer group for men who were struggling with various kinds of addictions, one man finally expressed his anger toward life in general and God in particular. I invited him to tell Jesus about this. He bowed his head and began a long and formal litany of "Praise you" and "Thank you, Father" type phrases. Eventually I interrupted him and asked where all his anger had gone. He hardly noticed what he had done. He was so conditioned to address God as a humble supplicant that he did not have the language to express his true feelings to God.

Imaginative prayer can help us unlock our true emotions—our annoyances, frustrations, anger, and disappointments. When we honestly enter a scene with Jesus, we make space for these feelings to emerge, just as they would with any other person we trust.

The Psalms teach us to pray this way, often expressing deep anguish, even anger at God: "Why, Lord, do you stand far off? Why do you hide yourself in times of trouble?" (Psalm 10:1). Those words might sound strong to you but they may also be so familiar that they simply run off your back. Eugene Peterson renders this verse this way, to help us feel the anguish of the psalmist. "God, are you avoiding me? Where are you when I need you?" (*The Message*). The Psalms invite us to bring our actual emotional responses to God in prayer, the ones we are truly feeling. Can I trust God enough to be honest with him? God invites us to share the entire range of our emotions with him.

When a friend of mine brought desperate questions to Jesus in prayer, he was frustrated because Jesus seemed completely unconcerned. When he saw Jesus' joy in a particular scene he was praying with, he immediately felt upset, ticked off, and disappointed with Jesus. "You don't even care about the things I care about," he told Jesus. He had been taught that he shouldn't feel angry with Jesus, but his imagination helped bring his actual emotional responses to the surface. Though he was extremely upset with Jesus in his life, he had been unable to access those feelings. Praying with his imagination helped him to be more honest with his feelings before God. In this place of honesty and vulnerability, Jesus longs to meet us.

Ignatian scholar Robert Egan writes that imaginative prayer produces "new possibilities and unexpected outcomes—outcomes that reveal something about the depths of the (pray-er's) heart."[5] These "unexpected outcomes" can come upon us quite intensely as an imagined scene takes us by surprise and reveals something about Jesus or ourselves. When we talk about these experiences with Jesus, we forge real trust and deeper intimacy in our relationship.

Our emotions can sometimes be deeply hidden within us, covered with layers of self-protection or shame and difficult to access. These hidden emotions can be revealed in prayer as we pay attention to how we are responding physically in an imagined scene. These external clues can guide us to the state of our heart. Without realizing it, we often hide ourselves from God, especially when shame is involved. As we encounter Jesus, these deeply hidden emotions have room to emerge. As Philip Sheldrake writes:

> In our thoughts we can rationalize, we can convince ourselves that we are not afraid or not angry. We recognize, though, that our actions often reveal our true state. In my real life, if I draw back, there is fear in me even if I try to convince myself there is not. So, too, with imaginative prayer. We find ourselves acting in the scene that is often closer to what is deeply true in us. This can be self-revealing; taken to prayer it can be an opportunity for real growth, change and intimacy.[6]

Our actions in an imaginative prayer experience can open a window into the hidden emotions that we find difficult to face. One friend admitted that she is sometimes physically afraid of Jesus in prayer, backing off from him as he approaches her. "It's almost like I'm scared of him coming," she shared and then began to cry. "I think he's going to ask me to do all these things. I'm scared of him requiring more of me than I have to give." Apart from this prayer experience, if you were to ask this woman if she was afraid of Jesus

5. Egan, "Jesus in the Heart's Imagination," 67.
6. Sheldrake, "Imagination and Prayer," 101.

she would have answered with an emphatic "No." She loved Jesus deeply. And yet the Spirit used her imagination to reveal the fear that was operating within her, which she felt in her resistance to Jesus approaching her in prayer. When she recognized and named her fear, she was freed to pray honestly and listen for Jesus' response to her.

While reflecting on the experience of watching Jesus being led out to Golgotha, another friend expressed surprise about his desire to reach out and touch Jesus' robe. "I just want to be close to him," he told me, on the verge of tears. This man rarely expressed emotion and was unused to speaking about his deep longing for God but through this prayer experience, he was able to articulate his love for Jesus in a way that profoundly moved him and drew him closer to Jesus.

Imaginative prayer will not necessarily lead us to answers to particular questions but will probably bring even more questions to the surface. Our desire is to encounter Jesus, express the reality of our emotions, and listen with the "eyes of your heart" (Ephesians 1:18) to what he is saying. As we notice how we are acting and feeling in imaginative prayer and then vulnerably express our longings and emotions to Jesus, our "trust" tree will be nurtured and strengthened so that we will be able to face any difficulties that lie ahead. Though we risk hearing only silence or experiencing hidden pain, Jesus invites us forward, and trust compels us to follow him.

In the next chapter, we will discuss the stage of surrender in our relationship with Jesus, but before we walk cautiously into that part of the journey, we will enter the well-known story of Mary, Martha, and Lazarus. We will approach the story as if we are entering it for the first time, inviting the Spirit to unveil our buried emotions and express the "truth in the inner parts" that we may not realize we have been hiding. We will enter the story at verse 17 in John 11 and pray through the narrative twice—once as Martha and again as Mary—so that we can experience it from both perspectives.

IMAGINATIVE PRAYER EXERCISE: MARY AND MARTHA (JOHN 11:17-36)

You are Martha and are grieving the death of your brother Lazarus. Take a few moments to feel the gravity of your loss and pain. Think about an actual loss in your life—the death of a loved one, the death of a long-held dream, or another painful experience of loss and sorrow.

You are in your house, and you hear someone in the street cry out that Jesus is coming. You jump up to go meet him. "Jesus is coming," you tell your sister, Mary, who is sitting by the front window. She doesn't respond or shift her gaze to look at you. "Jesus is coming!" you repeat. When Mary remains motionless, you slam the front door in frustration. *Let her stay at home! She has left me to grieve alone for the past four days!*

As you run toward Jesus on the road, you feel a burst of emotion that he did not arrive in time to heal Lazarus. Is it anger? Frustration? Confusion? You slow down as you approach him. His eyes light up when he sees you, but then immediately fill with sadness.

"Lord," you call out, "if you had been here, my brother would not have died." Jesus stops walking. You feel flooded with his tender compassion as he looks at you. As you draw closer to him you lower your head, ashamed of your outburst. "But I know that even now God will give you whatever you ask," you murmur.

Jesus wraps his arms around you. "Your brother will rise again," he says.

Your jaw tightens and you clench your fists. "I know—in the resurrection on the last day." You feel the anger rising inside you again. You don't care about the "last day." You are missing your brother right now.

"*I am* the resurrection," Jesus says gently, wrapping his hands around your fists. "I am the life." He rubs his fingers lightly across your clenched jaw. "Whoever believes in me will never die." He lifts your chin and looks into your eyes. "Do you believe this?"

"Yes, Lord," you say, and as the words leave your mouth, you feel a surge of wild, new hope. *Resurrection. Life. Never die.* "I believe."

Now take some time to listen to your inner responses. How are you feeling? What emotions are rising to the surface? Try not to edit anything. You might find that you respond quite differently than Martha does in the story. Allow your true feelings to emerge. What do you notice about Jesus in this moment?

∼

Return to the beginning of the story to pray it again as Mary.

You are in your house, sitting by the front window, grieving the death of your brother, Lazarus. Your sister, Martha, has just rushed away from the house to meet Jesus. You are so exhausted. Your limbs feel so heavy. When

Martha yelled that Jesus was coming, you couldn't even respond. You know she is angry with you, but you are too tired to move. You just want to sit here at home. You are tired of having so many people around telling you how sorry they are. You just want to be left alone. You feel empty, hollow, numb. You remember sitting often at Jesus' feet—there was nowhere you would rather be! But now you can't even bear to be near him—or even hear his name. You just want to sit in the darkness and disappear.

Suddenly Martha is standing next to you, saying your name, "Mary." She touches your shoulder. "Mary," she says again, then leans down and wraps her arms around you. Her arms feel warm and tender—not rigid and cold as they did earlier. You lean tentatively into her embrace. "The Teacher is here," she whispers. "He is asking for you." There is no bitterness in her voice. You look at her face and she is leaning toward you, smiling, her eyes full of light and life.

Jesus wants to see *you*! Jesus wants to talk with *you*! You feel a sudden burst of energy and jump up, then hug Martha tightly. You rush out of the house together to meet Jesus, outside the village at the place where Martha just left him. But as soon as you see Jesus standing there on the side of the road, all your emotions spill out and you begin to cry.

"Lord," you sob, "if you had been here, my brother would not have died."

Then you fall at Jesus' feet and weep. You have nothing to say.

Jesus touches your back. You look up at him. His eyes are red and puffy—he has been weeping as well. He leans his head against yours and says, "Mary, where have you laid him?" His voice breaks as he sobs. Then he pulls you to your feet, and you say, "Come and see." You lead him through your village, followed by a crowd of friends who have come to console you and your sister, toward the cave where you and Martha recently buried your brother.

As Jesus draws near the tomb, you see his pain expressed in his body. He stands there for several minutes.

Then he calls out, "Take away the stone."

Remain with Jesus in this moment and ask him to show you his desire for you, the sorrow he feels for the pain that you carry. Ask him to reveal his compassion to you—how he knows your pain and is moved by your sorrow. Now invite him to speak to you about something in your life that needs to be resurrected. Invite him to take away the stones that are blocking you from that new life.

CHAPTER 8

Surrendering to Jesus

"Father, if you are willing, take this cup from me;
yet not my will, but yours be done."

—Luke 22:42

SURRENDERING TO JESUS IS a part of our life in Christ from the very beginning of our journey. The initial act of saying "Yes" to the Lord is a kind of surrender—I am placing his life before my own, if only in small ways initially. But I am placing surrender at this later point in our journey because of the way surrendering to Jesus has manifested in my own life. All of these stages of the relationship journey are intertwined, and we will return to them again and again in different seasons of our lives and with different intensities. But as I have reflected on the journey of the disciples in the Gospels, I see Jesus leading them towards progressively deeper levels of commitment and surrender. First, he asks them to follow him, then he asks them to trust him, and once they come to see the full extent of his call upon their lives, he asks them to surrender themselves completely to the Father, trusting that he will lead them to life, even though death seems much closer on the horizon.

You have likely faced this kind of experience in your Christian life—the call to a new measure of commitment that requires you to let go at a whole new level. Or, as has more often been the case with me, you sense a longing to commit yourself and live a more fully surrendered life, but you feel troubled because you do not know how to do this. When we prayerfully imagine ourselves standing on this precarious cliff edge of surrender with Jesus, our decision takes on a much more visceral reality.

In the spiritual and emotional upheaval of losing a ministry job several years ago, I began to avoid my own pain through the use of pornography. It was hidden, I felt ashamed, but I did not take steps to move away from it. Quite inadvertently, Andrea discovered what I was doing and was devastated. I had betrayed her and she was crushed. My initial response was one of self-protection and evasion. I made excuses, minimized my actions, and accused her of overreacting. I was unwilling to face the depth of my betrayal. Several days went by. We both withdrew. In my mind I kept rehearsing my excuses and my self-protection—yes, it was sin but it was not *that* bad, others were far worse, can't we just get past this?

I was reading a book a few days later about sexual addiction and healing. I was feeling rather smug, facing my problem, learning about myself, or so I thought. But I was still hiding. The book recounted several stories of men caught up in addictive behavior and I was quick to compare myself to them, coming out much better, of course. I was about halfway through the book, still feeling rather self-righteous, when the Lord spoke to my heart, "*Dan, you are no different than these men. This is the direction you are heading.*" Immediately, I dropped the book and began weeping. The Lord's conviction was severe but true. It was an invitation to surrender. It enabled me to let go of all my self-protection and hiding, to face my shame, and to open myself to the love and forgiveness I so desperately needed. I picked up the book, returned to the beginning and read it again. It became a significant part of my healing.[1]

The decision to surrender is rarely easy. We hang on fiercely, fighting to the bitter end to keep ahold of ourselves and stay in control so we can keep our sense of identity intact. We grasp our idols with reckless abandon, hoping that Jesus will not notice, or that he will let us continue along with a wink and a nod. Perhaps we can reach a negotiated peace agreement, we imagine, rather than a full-fledged surrender. But there is no peace agreement on the table. The only offer that Jesus makes is full and complete surrender. We acquiesce to such terms only when we know that our resources are gone, our strength is spent, and our future is hopeless on our own. Even so, to surrender takes immense trust in the one to whom we offer our lives. What we discover as we slowly open our clenched hands is the One who

---

1. The book was *False Intimacy* by Harry Schaumburg.

calls for our surrender is full of immense love and gratuitous mercy. As we fall into God we find we are falling into love.

SURRENDERING IN LOVE

Surrendering may be an act of giving up, releasing our firm grip on our control and self-protection. It may also look like allowing ourselves to be loved, surrendering to the invitation to believe that we are deeply lovable. Either way, surrendering requires a level of trust and love that is difficult to find in most relationships in our lives. We often choose to protect our hearts from this level of vulnerability rather than expose them to possible harm. We may know a measure of this dynamic within our marriage or with intimate friends. There may only be one or two people whom we would trust enough to offer ourselves fully and completely in a "surrendering" way. It simply requires too much risk and vulnerability.

Yet we may have tasted it in our lives when we put the needs of our spouse or friend above our own. When we put ourselves in another's hands, we trust that this person truly has our best interests at heart, loves us unconditionally, and will not hurt us or abandon us. Marriage is supposed to be the arena for nurturing this kind of love and mutual surrender. As Paul says in 1 Corinthians 7:4, "The wife does not have authority over her own body but yields it to her husband. In the same way, the husband does not have authority over his own body but yields it to his wife." This kind of relationship can only be lived out if both the husband and the wife surrender to one another in love, trusting they are completely safe and cared for by the other. Because they trust they will not be abused, used, or manipulated for personal gain, they are willing to risk self-sacrificial love for one another. Such a marriage relationship, where "the two shall become one," is meant to point us toward the immense love that God the Father has for all of his children.

With a close friend, you may have tasted what it is like to surrender to one another in love. Perhaps your friendship has gone through a relational crisis, and you have learned to forgive and be forgiven in ways that bind you closer together. Perhaps you have gone through an intense life or death experience together, and you have had to rely on each other or be willing to sacrifice your life for one another. Such acts of surrender intimately forge people together.

This kind of surrender in our human relationships is rare because we are far too attached to our own desires and needs. We think of the above passage in 1 Corinthians as impossible and unrealistic. Elsewhere, when Paul tells us to "value others above yourselves" (Philippians 2:3), we roll our eyes because we cannot imagine how we could ever live that way consistently. It is just not how real life works. So we retreat to looking after ourselves, protecting our hearts, afraid of the inevitable pain of rejection and hurt. We negotiate "calculated agreements" with others because we recognize that surrender will cost us something that we may not be prepared to pay. When we turn our eyes toward Jesus, though, and listen to his call to surrender, we see before us someone who has already surrendered to his Father, already laid down his life for us. Like all stages of the spiritual journey, Jesus goes before us—and invites us to follow him.

NOT MY WILL: JESUS' STRUGGLE TO SURRENDER

In chapter 7, we looked at Mark's account of Jesus inviting his friends to turn with him toward the cross as they are walking to Caesarea-Philippi (Mark 8:31–38). Up to this point in their relationship with Jesus, they have been moving along an upward trajectory, witnessing Jesus' astounding power of healings, incredible miracles, and inspiring teaching—all increasing his glory and fame. Then Jesus says that it is time to let all of that go. It is time to surrender—even unto death.

In Matthew's account of this story, Peter responds to this sobering news by blurting out, "Never, Lord" (Matthew 16:22). Peter was profoundly attached to the upward mobility he and his friends had been enjoying with Jesus. Surrender was not his plan for Jesus at all, never mind for himself. Though he likely felt he was following Jesus honestly and courageously, he was tightly holding on to his own plans. This "way of the cross" was a bridge too far. It seemed ridiculous and too full of danger. Why would anyone choose such a course? We too, like Peter, are steeped in a world that promises a path of success, fulfillment and flourishing, a life of upward mobility. Surrender does not fit that paradigm, so we resist, offer alternative options, anything but letting go. Though Peter is unable to surrender in that moment, Jesus does not reject him. He rebukes him, harshly, and then reiterates the invitation to surrender. "Whoever wants to be my disciple must deny themselves and take up their cross and follow me" (Mark 8:34).

This invitation to surrender is not something new in Jesus' teaching. He has been hinting at it all along. When Jesus teaches his disciples to pray, he comes quickly to a prayer of surrender. "Our Father in heaven, hallowed be your name, your Kingdom come, *your will be done*" (Matthew 6:9–10 emphasis added). The relinquishment of our will to the Father, a deep and significant surrender, is central to Jesus' teaching and at the heart of our relationship with God.

Jesus lives out this prayer of surrender when he enters the garden of Gethsemane in the final hours of his life. There, he experiences extreme anguish. In Matthew's report, Jesus' tells his friends, "My soul is overwhelmed with sorrow to the point of death. Stay here and keep watch with me" (Matthew 26:38). Then Jesus moves off to pray alone, and Matthew records both his struggle and his surrender: "My Father, if it is possible, may this cup be taken from me. Yet not as I will, but as you will" (Matthew 26:39).

I grew up with this story and heard many sermons about Jesus' humanity, his anguish, and his struggle portrayed in Gethsemane. I also heard a lot about how the disciples fell asleep and how we should not be like them! But I never understood the immensity of Jesus' struggle with his Father until I entered this story imaginatively and noticed Jesus' movements. I placed myself there, with Peter, James, and John, and carefully watched all that was happening. After Jesus' initial struggle in prayer, he returns to find the disciples sleeping. He talks with them briefly and then goes "away a second time" (Matthew 26:42). He had come to the place of surrender in his first prayer, but now seems to back away from this, asking the Father to take away the cup of suffering. But once again, he acquiesces to his Father's will. When he returns and finds his friends asleep again, he "went away once more and prayed the third time, *saying the same thing!* (Matthew 26:44, emphasis added). Jesus retreats from his surrender a *third time* and prays for another way, another "negotiated agreement," before he once again comes to the place of full surrender: "Not my will but yours be done." These words are so simple to say, simpler yet to read, and yet devastatingly difficult to live. Perhaps in these moments, Jesus remembered the temptation of Satan in the desert years before, insisting that Jesus did not need to suffer ("tell these stones to become bread," Matthew 4:3) or surrender to God ("All this I will give you if you bow down and worship me," Matthew 4:9). We all face these temptations as we wrestle with the prospect of surrendering. And this wrestling often takes a long time. We do not know how long Jesus wrestled in prayer that night but returning three times reveals the difficulty of letting go, even for him.

Though Peter and the other disciples struggled to understand Jesus' call to surrender, Paul clearly outlines all the attachments he needed to surrender in order to follow Jesus fully. In Philippians 3, Paul lists them: his position as a righteous Hebrew, his blameless lifestyle, his pedigree of being from the "right" tribe. For the sake of Christ, he lets it all go, saying, "I consider everything a loss because of the surpassing worth of knowing Christ Jesus my Lord" (Philippians 3:8). Surrender will look different for each of us, but it often requires us to relinquish our deeply held attachments, ego, status, career, and hopes for the future. Our hearts may desire to surrender, but our flesh struggles to let go of all the things we think we need to survive. We may desire to know the "power of Jesus' resurrection" (Philippians 3:10a) in our life but be unwilling to "participate in his suffering" (Philippians 3:10b; 2 Corinthians 1:5–7). The process of surrendering to Jesus can be painful because it does not protect us from suffering, but ultimately, it releases us into greater freedom and life-giving joy.

In the following exercise, we will enter a story that helps us receive Jesus' powerful love. We need to know the depth of his love for us before we can contemplate surrendering to him. This exercise helps us see and receive the immensity of Jesus' humble love for us. Many of us struggle to surrender fully to Jesus because we are not quite sure of his love. Our wounds run deep. We do not fully trust him not to harm us, accuse us, or condemn us. We may know the theological truths about Jesus' love but this exercise helps us to enter into it with our bodies as well as our minds.

IMAGINATIVE PRAYER EXERCISE: RECEIVING THE HUMBLE LOVE OF JESUS (JOHN 13)

You are gathered with Jesus and your friends with whom you have been working for three years. You have seen amazing things on your journey together: blind people receiving sight, crippled people leaping to their feet, some people have even been brought back to life after dying! You have also felt God's power moving within you as you have prayed for people and seen them healed and delivered from demons.

You are getting ready to have dinner with Jesus and your friends. You are all reclining alongside a low table that is being filled with food by servants. Look around the room for a moment. What do you notice about the room? What is everyone around you doing? What are people talking about? How close are you to Jesus? What do you notice about him?

Suddenly, Jesus gets up from the table and moves toward the door. He takes off his outer cloak, picks up the basin of water used for washing feet, pours water into it and ties a towel around his waist. The room grows silent as people begin to notice what Jesus is doing. All eyes watch him intently. What do you whisper to your friends as you see this? The house servants are supposed to wash feet. What is Jesus doing? How do you feel as you watch him?

He crosses to the far side of the room, leans down by one of your friends, and begins to wash their feet. The room is silent but for the gentle splashing of the water in the basin. How does your friend respond? What are the others doing?

Jesus finishes and moves to the next person. He does not move quickly. He is slow and deliberate. He takes each foot and washes it, looking up into people's faces. Jesus moves around the table from person to person. How do you feel as you watch Jesus? As you imagine Jesus approaching you, you may want to take off your shoes and socks to make yourself ready to receive him.

Jesus now comes to you. How are you positioned when Jesus stops in front of you? How do you picture Jesus? What does he say as he touches your feet? How do you respond?

If you find yourself resisting, pay attention to what you are feeling. Can you tell him what you are feeling? What do you want to say to Jesus? How does he respond to you?

As Jesus dries off your feet, is there anything more you would like to say to him? Let this scene fade as you continue to sit with Jesus.

SURRENDER AS THE FOUNDATION OF LIFE

In *God's Good World*, Jonathan Wilson reveals how the act of surrendering is not unique to our spiritual development but is fundamental to all of life. He writes:

> Just as God the Father, the Son, and the Holy Spirit live in con-tinual self-giving and self-receiving, so also do all created things live . . . At the present time, this giving and receiving in order to be living has been upended in the world, which is in rebellion against God's rule and God's way of life. The world is now ruled not by

giving and receiving but by taking and keeping. The word for taking and keeping is *death* . . . When we take and keep we are not
living but dying.[2]

Because self-giving surrendering is part of the created order, our resistance
to this way of life is a core feature of our fallenness. We are now bent toward self-preservation, but real life comes through sacrifice and surrender.
Psychologist and spiritual director David Benner expresses this succinctly,

> Paradoxically, the abundant life promised us in Christ comes not
> from grasping but from releasing. It comes not from striving but
> from relinquishing. It comes not so much from taking as from giv-
> ing. Surrender is the foundational dynamic of Christian freedom.[3]

Perhaps Jesus' mother, Mary, knew this intuitively when she was confronted by the angel at the announcement of Jesus' conception. She knew
that to surrender was to choose life. When I refuse to surrender, I am not
choosing life but death. I am choosing myself rather than God. The genius
of the evil one is that he has led us to believe the exact opposite, so we keep
hanging on rather than letting go.

SURRENDER AS A KIND OF DEATH

It seems utterly foolish in these days of personal autonomy and self-actu-
alization to think that surrendering is the pathway to anything but failure
and defeat. Of course, it *is* a kind of defeat, but a defeat of the prison that
we have created around our own hearts. Benner writes, "Only surrender to
something or someone bigger than us is sufficiently strong to free us from
the prison of egocentricity"[4] We need to be rescued from the prison of our
own making.

Surrendering can often feel like a kind of death, and none of us will
choose death easily. It is a death to our ego-driven selves, the desire to rule
ourselves without God. We have been seeking life through all our attachments—the idols we nurture, everything from material things to emotional
states to spiritual experiences. Jesus invites us to let go of all these attachments and follow him so that we can discover a life of freedom and belong-
ing. Our attachments can be so deeply ingrained in how we view ourselves

2. Wilson, *God's Good World*, 109, 113.

3. Benner, *Surrender to Love*, 60.

4. Benner, *Surrender to Love*, 10.

that we may wonder if there really *can* be life without them. When we surrender these things, it can feel as if we are entering a place of utter darkness and annihilation. Think of losing your family, your entire savings, your sight, your ability to walk, your intelligence. Although these are all good gifts, they are not the *sources* of life, and yet we cling to them as if they are.

When we surrender our idols, we release our need to be the god of our own lives. Sadly, if we're honest, we often do not *want* to surrender to God. We want to *be* God ourselves. We want to find our own way, achieve our own successes, become somebody in this world! But Jesus knows that *our* way will only lead to death, so he keeps asking us to surrender. When we resist, we reveal that what we *really* want is to have Jesus as a life coach or a personal trainer who will help us fulfill our goals and live out our full potential. Michael Casey, the Australian contemplative, calls this our resistance to the "dethronement of self."[5] Releasing these deeply held attachments is humbling and frightening.

When we face Jesus as he stretches out his hands to receive all that we are desperately clinging to, we will continue to clutch ever more tightly unless we know that Jesus loves us with an everlasting love and we can trust his purposes for our life.

SURRENDER AS LETTING GO

The notion of surrendering can be rather amorphous. What does it look like to surrender? Am I supposed to quit my job? Am I supposed to move away and change everything? Our imagination can be our ally here, helping us to "concretize" our letting go. Henri Nouwen found the image of a trapeze artist letting go of the bar in order to be caught by a partner wonderfully enlightening. I have never been on a trapeze bar, but this image of a trapeze artist letting go of the bar and free flying through the air, trusting a partner to make the catch, grabs me at a deeply visceral level. Nouwen describes the conversation where he first learned of the skill of the trapeze artist.

> One day, I was sitting with Rodleigh, the leader of the troupe, in his caravan, talking about flying. He said, 'As a flyer, I must have complete trust in my catcher. The public might think that I am the great star of the trapeze, but the real star is Joe, my catcher. He has to be there for me with split-second precision and grab me out of the air as I come to him in the long jump.'

5. Casey, *Toward God*, 5.

'How does it work?' I asked.

'The secret,' Rodleigh said, 'is that the flyer does nothing and the catcher does everything. When I fly to Joe, I simply have to stretch out my arms and hands and wait for him to catch me and pull me safely over the apron behind the catchbar.'

'You do nothing!' I said, surprised.

'Nothing,' Rodleigh repeated. 'The worst thing the flyer can do is to try to catch the catcher. I am not supposed to catch Joe. It's Joe's task to catch me. If I grabbed Joe's wrists, I might break them, or he might break mine, and that would be the end for both of us. A flyer must fly, and a catcher must catch, and the flyer must trust, with outstretched arms, that his catcher will be there for him.'[6]

This powerful image of letting go and trusting the Divine Catcher to catch us gives us a profound picture of what it looks like to surrender to Jesus and free fall into God.

Take a moment and imagine yourself as a trapeze artist, letting go of the catchbar of your life, trusting that you will be caught by Jesus. Notice how firmly you are holding the bar. Imagine yourself swinging back and forth, seeing Jesus getting ready to catch you. What do you feel as you swing? When you are ready, let go. How do you feel as you free fall? Now imagine yourself being caught in the arms of Jesus, swinging freely into the arc of new life and freedom.

We can only respond to the invitation to surrender to Jesus and let go of ourselves as we come to know and trust the depth of the Father's love for us. Our ego-driven self makes it nearly impossible to do this. We have learned to trust only ourselves. We need the Spirit, the one who calls out "Abba, Father" within us, to give us the courage and power we need to surrender, to let go. This process takes a long time as we live with Jesus and invite love and intimacy to grow between us. We will need to return again and again to those words of Scripture that reassure us of the depth of God's love, passages like those at the end of Chapter 1. These "living words" provide us the power to "give ourselves to God with all the loving abandon which he gives himself to us."[7] Those moments will arrive in your life where you will find you are able to say, "Ok, Lord, I will do whatever you ask of me. I belong to you. I am not my own."

Some years ago, I journeyed through the Transfiguration story with an imaginative prayer group. At the end of this story, Jesus and the disciples

6. Nouwen and Jonas, "Henri Nouwen Writings," lines 11–25.

7. Finley, The Awakening Call, 19.

walk down the mountain and meet with a crowd who have gathered there. The leader encouraged us to speak freely with Jesus about the experience we had just had on the mountain. As I expressed my gratitude for the amazing ways God was meeting me, I sensed Jesus saying, "I will do whatever it takes to forge a love bond between us, Dan. Will you?"

MY STRUGGLE TO LET GO

I am constantly aware of the ways I hang on to my life, out of fear, shame, and pride. I internally "hedge my bets," just in case following Jesus does not work out. I struggle to surrender, fight to keep control over my life by trying harder and pushing forward in all the places where Jesus is inviting me to let go. I am afraid of being vulnerable because I do not want to stand naked or empty-handed before God. I want to find something good about myself that I can offer to God, some measure of success, some good character quality, some profound insight, some fragment of humility. I want God to like me, so I dig around trying to find something that will make me more attractive. But Jesus tells me to let go of all my striving.

When I was on a silent retreat some time ago, I knew I had to face this question of surrender. I wanted to lay down my life fully to Jesus, but I also felt an intense resistance to doing so. I knew that I could deceive myself into pretending that I was surrendering my life while secretly holding back my heart. I could say the words but I did not know how to proceed honestly from my heart. I was stuck once again in thinking that I had to surrender completely and unequivocally but I did not know how to do that.

Then I thought about my marriage and realized that I had committed to love and cherish my wife, Andrea, at the beginning of our marriage but that I had not really known how to do that. My commitment to her was not that I loved her fully when we began our life together but that I was choosing to learn how to love her fully, that I was committing to moving in the direction of love. So, too, with God. I did not need to know how to surrender to God completely before I did it. I just needed to "get married" and begin the process of learning how to release my grip on my life and trust Jesus to catch me.

I felt the need to take some action to express my desire and decision to take this step with Jesus. I wanted to seal the memory of this prayer in my body, mind, and heart. There was a chapel at the retreat center where I was staying so I went down in the middle of the night, stood in front of the imagined marriage altar, and prayed this prayer. "It is to you, Jesus, that I choose to lay down my life. I do not know how to do that. But here I am, committed to finding out with you." I wept as I admitted that I did not know how to surrender my life—and often did not even want to—but was trusting Jesus to teach me. Now, when I am tempted to take back control over my life, which happens all the time, I often recall that day, remembering that marriage ceremony in front of the altar, and I ask Jesus to help me surrender to him once again.

A friend recently introduced me to the "Prayer of Abandonment" by Charles de Foucauld, an early twentieth-century monastic, who was the founder of the Little Brothers and Sisters of Jesus. I often pray this to remind myself of the commitment I made that day at the altar.

> Father, I abandon myself into your hands;
> do with me what you will.
> Whatever you may do, I thank you.
> I am ready for all, I accept all.
> Let only your will be done in me, and in all your creatures.
> I wish no more than this.
> O Lord, into your hands I commend my soul;
> I offer it to you with all the love of my heart,
> for I love you, Lord, and so need to give myself into your hands
> without reserve, and with boundless confidence,
> for you are my Father.[8]

When I told my spiritual director about this prayer, I was wisely encouraged to add, "And I can't do any of this on my own. Please help me!" We are not heroes in this journey, but weak vessels expressing our honest longings and limitations to a loving and merciful God.

THE ONGOING STRUGGLE TO SURRENDER

The ongoing task of surrendering to Jesus has been extraordinarily difficult for me. I often find myself succumbing to temptations to meet my own needs, prove myself worthy, and avoid suffering. My fear and pride keep me grabbing back the reigns of my life. As I continue to struggle, it helps me to remember that I am not surrendering to an idea or a set of principles but to the person of Jesus Christ. Douglas Steere writes, "If it is true that the deepest prayer at its nub is a perpetual surrender to God, then all meditations

8. Crossroads Initiative, "Prayer of Abandonment—Charles De Foucauld," line 4–18.

and specific acts of prayer might be seen as preparations and purifications to ready us for this never-ending yielding."[9] For me, this has meant telling Jesus more often than not, as I stand before him, face to face, that I cannot seem to loosen my grip on my life. I need his mercy, grace, and power to surrender.

Over the years, I have lived with the ongoing sense that I have been holding back from God, that if Jesus asked me to do certain things or release certain attachments I would be unwilling. This causes deep shame to well up within me. I have longed to surrender completely to Jesus but have felt powerless in seeking to overcome my fear and lack of trust. I was talking with a spiritual director about this dynamic, and he suggested that I pray with the story of the rich young ruler in Mark 10. During our conversation, he said, "The saddest part of that story is not that the man could not do what Jesus asked him to do—give away all his money—but that he turned and walked away. What if he had stayed? What if he had stayed and confessed his inability? What do you think Jesus would have done?"[10]

In this next imaginative prayer exercise, I invite you to enter the story of the rich young ruler. You may or may not have a sense of something specific that Jesus is asking you to surrender. Or you may sense that there would be something quite difficult for you to release if you were made aware of it. Before entering the story, we will begin by asking Jesus to reveal this attachment, if it exists, and then continue from there.

We will pray this story twice, once as it is written in Mark, and then a second time, allowing you to have a different response than the rich young ruler. I encourage you to engage your body by acting out the movements in this story as you open your heart to be led by the Spirit.

IMAGINATIVE PRAYER EXERCISE: THE RICH YOUNG RULER (MARK 10:17–22)

You are standing on a slight rise alongside a road watching Jesus talk and laugh with a group of children as you wait for a chance to speak with him. Look up and down this road. What do you notice about it? What do you notice about Jesus as you watch him with the children?

Slowly, the children disperse one by one, running off down the road or back to their mothers. Jesus stands up and begins to walk away with his

9. Steere in Thomas Merton, *Contemplative Prayer*, 13.

10. William Barry SJ, personal conversation, March, 2013.

disciples. This is your chance. You walk quickly to catch up with him. When you are close you call out,

"Jesus? May I speak with you?" He stops, turns, and looks at you. Do you meet his eyes or do you find yourself looking away? How do you feel when he looks at you?

Jesus waits for you to speak. You gather yourself and say, "What must I do to inherit eternal life? What am I supposed to do to please God?"

"What *have* you been doing?" he asks.

Think about all that you are doing as a Christian. You read your bible. You go to church. You pray. You try to tell others about Jesus. What other things do you do? As you tell Jesus about these things, what do you notice about him? Mark says that Jesus looked at the young man "and felt a love for him." Can you see Jesus looking at you like this? With love?

"Those things are all very good," Jesus responds. "One more thing I ask of you . . ."

You wait. What is he going to say? Does something specific come to mind that Jesus asks you to let go of? He asked the rich young man to sell all his possessions. What does Jesus say to you?

If you sense Jesus asking you to let go of something specific in your life, how do you feel about that? How do you want to respond?

Perhaps nothing comes to mind, yet you know there would be things Jesus could ask you to let go of, things that you hold very tightly, that would cause you to respond like the young man in this story. He turned and walked away. Imagine yourself doing that, your face downturned, your heart full of grief as you walk away.

What does it feel like to turn away from Jesus? Take a moment to act this out, physically turning and taking a few steps away from Jesus. How does your heart feel as you walk away? How does it feel in your body?

∽

Now, I invite you to pray the story a second time, but with a different response.

Place yourself again on the side of the road, waiting for Jesus to be finished speaking to the children. You approach him and ask your question. Recount again the things that you do for Jesus in your Christian life, praying, Scripture reading, other ministry you are involved in. Do not rush through it.

Jesus listens carefully to all you have to say. When you are finished he says,

"Those things are all very good. One more thing I ask of you . . ."

What comes to mind? Is there something you are clinging to that Jesus asks you to release to him? Perhaps nothing specific comes to mind but you know you are holding back from Jesus. This time do not turn and walk away. Face Jesus and look at him. What do you want to say to him? Can you express your feelings of helplessness? Can you ask him for strength? Can you confess your fears?

What else is in you to say to Jesus? You might want to say something like, "Jesus, I want to let go of this, but I can't seem to do it. Will you help me?" How does Jesus respond to you? Imagine, now, after Jesus has listened to you, that he says,

"Come, follow me."

Jesus knows where you are. He knows the struggles you are facing as you try to surrender to him. He is neither surprised nor disappointed. Imagine yourself following after him and his disciples as they continue down the road, leading you into the next stage of the journey.

~

After the rich young ruler walks away, Mark says that the disciples are "amazed" by Jesus' difficult words (Mark 10:24). This man was exactly the kind of person who should be first in line for God's kingdom, or so the disciples thought. His learning, his wealth, and his moral uprightness set him apart as a profoundly religious and pious man. The disciples say, in effect, "If this guy can't make it, what chance do the rest of us have?" Jesus answers them, "You're right. It is impossible. But all things are possible with God."

Our ability to surrender is not a litmus test. Jesus is not leading us to these moments expecting us to respond like good little disciples, ready to surrender all to him. Rather, he is inviting us to face our own poverty, recognize how our attachments imprison us, and ask Jesus to help us surrender. To surrender to Jesus is not our achievement. Anytime we loosen our grip on our lives and look to Jesus alone for the life we need, the victory belongs to him, not to us. When we humbly acknowledge this, he will give us the strength to continue following him.

CHAPTER 9

Dying with Jesus

"Whoever wants to be my disciple
must deny themselves and take up their cross and follow me.
For whoever wants to save their life will lose it,
but whoever loses their life for me and for the gospel will save it."

—Mark 8:34–35

I have been crucified with Christ and I no longer live, but Christ lives in me.

—Galatians 2:20

WE COME NOW TO that part of the journey that we would rather avoid altogether. When we first began to follow Jesus, we probably recognized, to some degree, that we were abdicating our right to lead our own lives. Rather than striking out on our own, we made the decision to trust Jesus to lead us to something good.

But now, looking up at the cross, we wonder if perhaps we were mistaken. The cross of Jesus stretches across the landscape of our faith with unrelenting, inescapable pressure. As Dietrich Bonhoeffer puts it:

> The cross is laid on every Christian. The first Christ-suffering which every man (sic) must experience is the call to abandon the attachments of this world. It is that dying of the old man which is the result of his encounter with Christ. As we embark upon

107

discipleship we surrender ourselves to Christ in union with his death—we give over our lives to death. Thus it begins; the cross is not the terrible end to an otherwise god-fearing and happy life, but it meets us at the beginning of our communion with Christ. When Christ calls a man, he bids him come and die.[1]

The "cross" that is "laid upon every Christian" is the relinquishment of our lives that so desperately try to make our own way without God. When we decide to follow Jesus, he calls us to lay down our attachments to the world—our expectations about our success and advancement and our desires for a good life—from the beginning of our relationship. Yet before we feel the unrelenting pressure of the cross on our shoulders, he slowly and graciously draws us into a friendship of love and trust so that we will be assured of his accompaniment when we eventually have to pick up our own cross and follow his path of suffering.

When the cross inevitably casts its shadows across our path, fear often rises up within us, and our hearts grow faint. It is easy to say the words, "I love you, Lord," or "I trust you, Father," until we, like Peter, come face to face with an angry mob. Like the disciples, we discover that the renovations our hearts require are far more drastic than we anticipated. My own fear of following Jesus to the cross is exposed by the internal temptations that often get the best of me—the forces of self-preservation that rise up strenuously within me to refuse the way of the cross. Through desperate machinations of my ego, I cling stubbornly to my own path rather than following Jesus on his. But to receive our new life in Christ, we first have to endure the death of our old, ego-driven selves.

At the cross, we not only face real pain and suffering, but also our inability to grasp the wisdom of following such a scandalous path. Paul strongly and succinctly reminds the Corinthians that a crucified Messiah is at the core of their faith—not some promise of spiritual nirvana or a steady diet of miraculous and spectacular gifts. "Jews demand signs and Greeks look for wisdom, but we preach Christ crucified: a stumbling block to Jews and foolishness to Gentiles" (1 Corinthians 1:22–23). Paul suggests that we react negatively to the cross because we want God to be powerful and wise, victorious, and successful. But the cross is a sign of degradation, humiliation, and suffering. Standing at the cross we recognize just how much we were hoping, like the first disciples, for something quite different: success, a glorious outcome, a win. The cross cuts across all our defenses, exposing

1. Bonhoeffer, *Cost of Discipleship,* 89.

all our attachments, and makes no sense. To our human reason and philosophical understanding, the cross is ridiculous and utterly foolish. As we prayerfully approach the passion narratives in this chapter, let us ask God to give us eyes to see, ears to hear, and hearts to receive what "dying with Jesus" will demand of us.

OUR RELATIONAL LIFE

Throughout our journey we have identified many similarities between our human friendships and our relationship with Jesus. After we meet new friends, we get to know them and may eventually learn to deeply trust some of them. With a few friends, we may discover what it means to surrender to one another in love. But our human relationships can only supply us with a shadow of understanding at this new stage, as there are probably only a few people in our lives for whom we would be willing to die—possibly a spouse, a child, or a friend we love dearly. Yet Jesus says, "Greater love has no one than this: to lay down one's life for one's friends" (John 15:13). Such a love is difficult to fathom, and few of us will ever have to let go of our life, with all our dreams and longings, for a friend.

But Paul sees the self-denial dynamic as central to the Christ-united life. He calls the church in Philippi to have the same relational attitude as Jesus, who *was* willing to lay down his life for others. He exhorts the Philippians to "value others above yourselves" and not to look "to your own interests but each of you to the interests of the others" (Philippians 2:3–5). When I read these passages that call us to deny ourselves and take up our cross, I quickly think of all the caveats around relational manipulation and enmeshed codependency. While these considerations are valid, the demand stands. Jesus' call is to "come and die."

"I WILL DIE FOR YOU!"

As time passes in the Gospel narratives, the disciples begin to realize that Jesus is in more and more danger. They see the anger of the religious leaders. They recognize that Jesus is risking his life to continue his mission. After Peter's proclamation at Caesarea Philippi (Mark 8:27–30), Jesus begins telling his friends that he will be rejected and killed—and that he will rise again on the third day. While the disciples struggle to understand what

Jesus is saying, both Thomas and Peter courageously voice their willingness to follow Jesus, even unto death.

John 11 begins with the news that Lazarus, a close friend of Jesus, is acutely sick. When Jesus hears about Lazarus, he does not rush to be with him but remains where he is for two more days. Then he announces that they will return to Bethany to be with Lazarus. The disciples know that it is dangerous for Jesus to be seen so close to Jerusalem, so they begin to argue with Jesus saying, "Rabbi, a short while ago the Jews tried to stone you, and yet you are going back?" (John 11:8). Jesus responds to their fears, "Lazarus is dead," he says, "let us go to him." Then Thomas steps forward and declares, "Let us also go, that we may die with him."

Take a few minutes to pause now and reflect on this moment in the story. Later, three days after the crucifixion, Thomas doubts that Jesus is alive as the others proclaim. He was not in the room when Jesus first appeared to the disciples and he cannot fathom it. For this, he has been branded with the unhappy reputation of "doubting Thomas." Yet, on this day, hearing Jesus declare that Lazarus has died, Thomas is the one who steps forward and confidently says he is willing to follow Jesus to the bitter end, even to his own death. His bravado and courage here are note-worthy, but ultimately short-lived. After Jesus is arrested, when the cross is looming, Thomas and all the other disciples scatter and flee to protect themselves, leaving Jesus alone. He completely fails to live up to his bold promise.

Peter has his own moment of steely resolve. After the disciples eat their last meal with Jesus, they walk together to the Garden of Gethsemane and Jesus tells them that they will all abandon him that very night. Peter objects, saying, "Even if all fall away on account of you, I never will" (Matthew 26:33). Like Thomas, Peter courageously steps forward and proclaims his love and loyalty to Jesus. Thomas is likely nodding his head in agreement behind him.

Jesus turns and looks at him and speaks with devastating specificity, "Truly I tell you, this very night, before the rooster crows, you will disown me three times" (Matthew 26:34). Upon hearing this, perhaps Peter remembers that earlier rebuke from Jesus ("Get behind me, Satan"), but he is not deterred. Like Thomas, he believes he has it within him to follow Jesus to his death. He stands his ground. "Even if I have to die with you," he declares, "I will never disown you" (Matthew 26:35).

Jesus says nothing. He allows Peter's declaration to hang in the air. The scene shifts. The disciples follow Jesus into the garden. Minutes later, perhaps an hour or two, Peter's resolve is tested, but when he is confronted with the prospect of standing with Jesus in the face of death, he fails him. "I don't know the man!"

You and I are Thomas and Peter. We may feel the deep resolve to remain with Jesus and never leave his side, to follow him to the end. We may pronounce this conviction in myriad ways—through prayer, worship, silent adoration. In our prayer journey, we have imagined following, trusting, and surrendering to Jesus. Perhaps we have known moments of courage, even surrender, as we proclaim our love for Jesus. We have laid down our lives in order to follow him. But, like Thomas and Peter, most of us falter when faced with suffering and death.

In the wake of our own failure we turn our eyes to Jesus, recognizing that *his* death and *his* cross is the foundation for ours. He is led in the story, in chains and humiliation, to Golgotha where he will die. Everyone leaves him, except John, the beloved disciple, his mother Mary, Mary Magdalene, and a few other women. All his other friends—those whom he called, befriended, taught, and loved—desert him and leave him alone, too afraid to follow him to the hill where he will die.

We do not know the inner state of Jesus as he followed the path to his own death, but we can hear his immense suffering in his excruciating cry, '*My God, my God, why have you forsaken me?*" Somehow, this is the wisdom of God. This Cross. This defeat. This death. His friends have scattered because they cannot comprehend death as the place of victory, suffering as the place of redemption. To see their long-hoped-for Messiah beaten, humiliated, and dying on a cross is a complete scandal.

To die with Jesus is to stand where John and Mary Magdalene stood, allowing ourselves to see and experience what they experienced, allowing the power of this event to seep into our bones. We do so in our poverty, recognizing that even to stand here requires the Father's mercy and courage. We cannot follow Jesus on this cruciform path unless he enables us to do so. It is not in us.

In the following imaginative prayer exercise, we will enter the courtyard outside the high priest's house just after Jesus has been arrested in Gethsemane. Praying with this story can help us to be honest with ourselves about our fears of following Jesus wherever he is leading us. As you prayerfully enter this scene, ask God to give you eyes to see and a heart to receive the power and reality of Peter's experience as well as your own. This can be a difficult story to pray with so, before you begin, invite the Spirit to help you remain present to the scene as it unfolds before you and to reveal your heart to you.

IMAGINATIVE PRAYER EXERCISE: THE COURTYARD (MATTHEW 26:69–75)

You are standing in the courtyard of the high priest's house. You can still hear the laughter of the band of soldiers who arrested Jesus in the garden, but you can no longer see them. You glance through the gates leading into the inner courtyard, hoping for a glimpse of Jesus. He is not there. You sit in the shadows of a small fire with a few others, hoping not to be noticed. Your heart is pounding and your palms are sweating. You are afraid that someone will recognize you as one of Jesus' friends. You try to hide your face.

Your throat aches as you remember the dinner you shared together earlier—his baffling words about his body being bread, his blood being wine. You remember the sick jolt you felt when you realized that Judas had slipped away. You remember hearing Jesus' moan and cry as he prayed in the garden. You tried to stay awake, but your eyes were so heavy. You remember the disgust you felt when you recognized Judas emerging from the shadows, flanked by soldiers wielding swords. Then the confused and angry shouting. Your gut churns as you remember the soldier's ear—if only you hadn't missed! But no, your face burns as you remember how Jesus' eyes flashed at you as he turned and healed the man.

You clench your hands into fists as you remember how the soldiers pushed and shoved Jesus. Anger begins to rise within you. You look up. Your eyes dart across the scene before you. There are others close by. You strain to hear the hushed conversation but can only catch mumbles and coughs.

"You! You there!" A girl's voice. You look up. "You also were with Jesus of Galilee," she says, pointing at you. Everyone turns to look at you. The conversation stops. Silence. Eyes on you.

You swallow quickly. Before you know what you are saying you blurt out, "I don't know what you're talking about." You jump to your feet and push your way through the crowd that has gathered, keeping your head down, trying to hide in the shadows by the gate.

You look back hoping no one is following you. The courtyard is full of people. It feels like everyone is looking at you. You pull a shawl over your head and keep your head down as you push your way through the crowd.

Suddenly, you feel someone grab your cloak. "This one was with Jesus of Nazareth, too," a voice sneers. You freeze, then spin around to find several people staring at you. You look into the face of the one who spoke. He gives you a rough shake, his grip tightening.

"I don't know the man!" you stammer, pulling away from him. Did you shout it or was it a whisper?

The man releases your cloak with a grunt. The group moves away slowly. But then one of them stops and turns back toward you. "Hey," he yells, "You *must* be with Jesus. Your accent gives you away. You're from Galilee." Your heart starts pounding even faster now. You back away and press yourself into the crowd, nearly tripping as you spin and crash into others standing nearby. Your anger erupts. "Leave me alone!" You call curses down upon yourself. You are about to say more, your mind is filling with raging words, accusing words, fighting words. But before they come spilling out . . . a rooster crows. You freeze. Looking up, there, across the courtyard, Jesus. He is looking at you.

As your eyes meet his, what do you see? What do you feel? Remain in the scene for a few minutes, paying close attention to what comes to you.

DYING WITH JESUS

What does it really mean to die with Jesus? He alone is the author of our salvation so it does not mean that we are joining him in his atoning work. We will spend some time contemplating the cross in this chapter, but first we must recognize that we will experience many small "deaths" as we follow the way of Jesus. Suffering and pain come into our lives in myriad ways. Eugene Peterson says, "Much as we try to get out of it or find a way around it there is simply no following of Jesus that does not involve suffering and rejection and death. No exceptions."[2] Jesus warns his friends that they must take up their own crosses and follow him, something they would have understood as a path of suffering, Though this path might lead to physical death for some, Jesus locates the way of the cross in the context of self-denial, where we face suffering and relinquish our self-focused grasp on life.

Jesus says, "Whoever wants to be my disciple must deny themselves and take up their cross and follow me" (Mark 8:34). Following Jesus entails the death of all that is in us that seeks its own way independent of Jesus. All of us have elements within us that we are loathe to let go of, things we think

2. Peterson, *Jesus Way,* 178.

we need for survival. The attachments in our lives can be endless. But when Jesus asks us to let go of ourselves and follow him to the cross we discover that we are not in need of a re-education plan, or a behaviour modification scheme, but rather a total renewal of our hearts. The prophet Ezekiel expresses it this way: "I will give you a new heart and put a new spirit in you; I will remove from you your heart of stone and give you a heart of flesh" (Ezekiel 36:26).

Paul describes this transformation as taking off the old self and putting on the new (Colossians 3:9–10). This is a progressive process of transformation, but its *telos*, its end result, is already established in us in Christ. Mysteriously, we have *already* died with Christ (Romans 6:6) and yet whatever the particular experiential nature of this "dying" and "putting off" might be in our lives, it will feel like a kind of death. We might be tempted to think that surrendering and setting aside our selfish heart will bring some level of consolation, as if God needs to bless us when we let go. But this was not true for Jesus. He let go in Gethsemane and was led to the cross, seemingly an abject failure to all those looking on. Just as he was left to wait upon the Father, we, too, are cast upon the mercy of the Father to breathe life back into us. There is no turning back. As Bonhoeffer writes, "the door is shut—and can only be opened from the outside."[3]

When we deny ourselves, we do not simply allow others to get their way or pleasantly invite others to go before us in line. The self that Jesus invites us to relinquish is the life we have come to rely upon. We are deeply attached to this self, which taunts us with the promise that we can make our own way, and we do not need to suffer in order to follow Jesus because there is a better, more comfortable "spiritual" path to follow—one that will not require us to die. We have believed the serpent's lie that we can "be like God" and choose to follow our own path. But Jesus tells us, "I am the Way," and his way includes the Cross. When we refuse to deny ourselves, we are choosing ourselves over God. Thomas Merton describes it this way, "Love demands a complete inner transformation . . . And this involves a kind of death of our own being, our own self. No matter how hard we try we resist this death."[4] In order to become like Jesus, we must die to ourselves.

Our resistance to denying ourselves and following Jesus can be profound and surprising. We may *believe* in Jesus and commit our lives to following him, but our resistance often resides at a much deeper place

3. Bonhoeffer, *God is in the Manger,* 13.
4. Merton, *Wisdom of the Desert,* 18.

within us, a place that can be hard to articulate or even recognize. As Peter discovered in the courtyard the evening Jesus was arrested, the tentacles of our attachments are deeply entrenched within us. Imaginative prayer can help us notice and face our resistance by concretizing our often hidden and elusive resistance to self-denial. Our hearts are revealed in prayer, and, as we listen, we receive the invitation to offer them to Jesus.

THE JESUS WAY

Suffering and death are at the heart of the Jesus way, but most of us do not want to admit this. Like the Corinthian church, we need Paul to remind us that at the center of our faith is a *crucified* Messiah. While following Jesus will lead us to healing, joy, and an abundant life, Paul does not say he preaches Christ the Healer, or Christ the Gift Giver. No. It is Christ the Crucified One he preaches. Why this emphasis? Thousands of books have been written trying to answer that question so we are not going to answer it here in a few sentences, but it is important to reflect on the meaning of the cross for our journey with Jesus.

I came upon this sentence recently: "We think it was the resurrection that was the miracle but the early Fathers said it was Jesus' death that was the miracle. It is not in the character of God to die!"[5] Though the disciples experienced the pain of their friend and master being cruelly crucified on a Roman cross and then three days later felt the exuberance of seeing him again, they were not yet aware of the full significance of these events. In the days and years that followed, they would come to understand that Jesus was God incarnate, that the creator of the universe had chosen to take on the form of finite and sinful humanity and had willingly surrendered to a cruel, humiliating, and degrading death. Fleming Rutledge writes, "Crucifixion was specifically designed to be the ultimate insult to personal dignity, the last word in humiliating and dehumanizing treatment."[6] Jesus endured this so that he could enter into the darkest human heart, taking on the fullness of evil by surrendering to death. When we contemplate the cross with Jesus, we know that God himself is hanging there in ignominy. This is difficult to

---

5. I do not have a reference for this quote.

6. Rutledge, *Crucifixion,* 78. Most depictions of Jesus on the cross have been sanitized from what the actual event would have been like. Jesus would have been hung naked, publicly scorned, and humiliated. Rutledge gives a brief yet devastating description of crucifixion on pp. 93–96.

fathom. The author of life enters into its opposite in order to free us from its clutches. This is the extent to which God has gone in order to release us from the bondage of sin, shame, and guilt.

Jesus defeats death by dying, taking on the sin he hates so that we can be released from its curse in our lives—all our lust, laziness, greed, rebellion, whatever is holding us in bondage. And he does all of this out of *love!* When we reflect on our personal sin, we can often see the cross through a lens of punishment rather than love. While Jesus defeated sin on the cross, God was acting on our behalf in love, taking on suffering in order to free us into life.

AN EMPTY CROSS?

Most Christian churches will have a cross on display. The cross is the quintessential symbol of our faith, the place where the victory over death was won. In most Protestant churches the cross is empty to symbolize that the work of Christ has been completed. Jesus is raised and alive today. But the cross can easily morph into a symbol of victory while forgetting the suffering that accompanied that victory. If we never see Jesus hanging on that cross, we tend to forget all that he endured to free us from our bondage. When we enter the scene on Golgotha and stand with John and Mary at the foot of the cross, we resist the temptation to merely gain more *knowledge* of the cross without encountering the One who hung there. We stand and gaze upon Jesus who was flogged and beaten so that we could be released from bondage. He secured our freedom on that cross but we must not avoid the blood stains that wrought that freedom. Jesus did not free us through strength and power, but through suffering, weakness, and death. This is the Jesus' way.

In the following imaginative prayer exercise, we will put ourselves in Mary Magdalene's shoes. Scripture tells us remarkably little about Mary, but Matthew, Mark, and John all testify that she was present at the cross.[7] From Luke, we learn that Mary was delivered of "seven demons" by Jesus fairly early in his ministry (8:2) and after that she traveled with Jesus and the disciples "helping to support them out of their own means" (Luke 8:3). We can imagine that Mary has been growing in her own relationship with Jesus, along with the disciples, learning to love him and surrender herself

---

7. Luke mentions "women who had followed him from Galilee" but no names are mentioned.

to his love. She now finds herself standing here at this gruesome reality, her master hanging on a Roman cross.

While it is important to pay attention to our responses as we enter these prayer experiences, our focus should keep gravitating back toward Jesus. What is Jesus doing? What is Jesus saying? This is especially important at the cross. To help focus our attention on Jesus, we will walk through his seven last statements from the cross. Mary Magdalene would have heard these words as she stood there watching in horror her beloved friend and savior suffering unto death.

IMAGINATIVE PRAYER EXERCISE: MARY AT THE CROSS (LUKE 23:34, 43, 46; JOHN 19:26, 28, 30; MATT 27:46)

You stand shivering as you hold onto Mother Mary's arm. You feel John supporting her from the other side. She is so frail, her breathing so shallow.

You are exhausted after a long and excruciating night. As soon as you heard that Jesus had been arrested, you found his mother and rushed to the high priest's house to find out where they were taking him. You wept when you saw Jesus' bloodied face and beaten body. You and Mary clutched each other as you heard the crowd calling for his death. You followed him with heavy limbs as he carried his cross to this hill. As you watch him suffer, you remember each healing you witnessed and desperately wish he would do something now to save himself.

You look up. But it is too painful to see him suffering, so you look to Mary, then to John. They look back at you with shock and pain in their eyes. You hear Jesus groan and look up to see him pushing up against the wooden cross with his legs. You strain to hear him speak.

Father, forgive them, for they do not know what they are doing.

Your face burns with anger. Forgive them? *Forgive them?* How can he forgive his own executioners? Some of the soldiers standing around start to laugh and sneer at him. You don't want these monsters forgiven. You want him to do something to save himself!

"Aren't you the Messiah?" you hear someone say, tauntingly. "Save yourself and us!"

You realize it is one of the criminals hanging next to Jesus. You are ashamed to hear this man say the words you have been so desperately praying. *Save yourself, Jesus. Save yourself—how can we go on without you?*

Then the other criminal hanging on the other side of Jesus calls out, "Don't you fear God? We are getting what our deeds deserve. But this man has done nothing wrong." He looks at Jesus and weakly pleads, "Jesus, remember me when you come into your kingdom."

You watch Jesus turn his head towards the man. His eyes are full of compassion.

Truly I tell you, today, you will be with me in paradise.

You continue looking at Jesus' face, the blood, the tears. Mary leans heavily against you and shudders. You tighten your grip on her arm and feel John wrap his arms around her shoulders. As she sobs, you see Jesus looking at his mother, then at John. Jesus' face contorts with pain as he pushes himself up again to speak.

Woman, here is your son. John, here is your mother.

Even in his pain he thinks of others rather than himself. You remember how he came close to you when everyone else abandoned you, how he did not care about his reputation.

You hear some commotion off to one side. You look over to see a group of soldiers laughing and shoving one another. One holds up Jesus' robe and several men stoop down and throw dice on the ground. A heavy soldier leaps up and punches the air with his fist, then grabs the robe. Your stomach turns. As John stiffens and lurches towards the men, Mary slumps to the ground. You grab John's arm, and he looks at you. *Stay,* you plead silently. *She needs us.* John wraps his arms around Mary's shoulders, lifts her, and holds her up on her feet.

As the soldiers disperse, you notice a group of temple priests and teachers of the law standing on the far side of the hill. One shouts, "He saved others but he can't save himself!" "Yes," another mocks, "He is the *King of Israel!* Let him come down from that cross and then we will believe him." The crowd laughs and murmurs. You feel like screaming.

Your legs are aching, your back is sore from supporting Mary, and you feel utterly exhausted. The minutes drag on. You slide to the ground, and John eases Mary beside you, then sits on her other side. You hold hands and look up at Jesus. When you see his bloodied, broken legs, you are wracked with guilt, and you begin to weep.

You sit together for hours, refusing to leave your master. Every now and then, he shifts to take a labored breath, The sky begins to darken. You feel that Jesus is weakening. Suddenly, his eyes open wide, and with a massive effort he pushes himself up, his legs shaking with the effort.

Eloi, eloi, lama sabachthani. My God, my God, why have you forsaken me?

Your heart pounds, and you draw in your breath in shock. You remember how he spoke about his Father in Heaven—*our* Father. You look over at Mary, then at John. Surely God would not abandon him?

Jesus swallows, then whispers weakly.

I am thirsty.

Someone takes a pole with a sponge and lifts it up to his lips. He sucks the sponge, then lets it fall away.

It is finished.

The silence bears down on you. It is heavy, thick. You feel your breath being sucked out of your body. The light is draining out of the sky. You feel numb, empty, and hollow, your body a brittle shell.

Then Jesus struggles to take another breath. His face contorts as he pushes against the cross. Then he cries out in a loud voice,

Father, into your hands I commit my spirit.

He collapses, and his head slumps against his chest. A curtain of darkness falls upon you, and you are hit with the unbearable weight of his absence. You clutch Mary and feel John's arms tighten around you.

Linger here for several moments. Do not rush away. What are you feeling? What is the prayer that rises up within you?

CHAPTER 10

Rising with Jesus

The disciples were together with the doors locked
for fear of the Jewish leaders.

—John 20:19

"I have seen the Lord!"

—John 20:18

HOLY SATURDAY

BECAUSE WE ARE ALREADY living on this side of the cross, it is tempting to move quickly from Good Friday to Easter Sunday. Our Savior is alive, and our hearts yearn to celebrate that reality anew. But the disciples had to wait for their joy. They, like us, had to live through the unfolding of time. It is easy to say that Jesus rose "after three days," but those three days must have been excruciating for Jesus' friends, feeling more like a lifetime. Can you imagine what they must have been feeling? Confused? Frightened? Angry?

The Gospels do not tell us very much about the disciples on this day. John's Gospel says that they are huddled together "with the doors locked for fear of the Jewish leaders" (John 20:19). They had scattered after Jesus' arrest but have come together now, afraid of what would happen next. It was a real possibility that the Romans or Jewish leaders would be looking for them in order to fully eradicate this fledgling little sect.

Each of the four Gospel writers takes a few sentences after the passion narrative to describe the burial of Jesus,[1] before moving to the resurrection. These texts invite us to join with the disciples as they live through these dark days, waiting in fear. Because these days after the crucifixion and before the resurrection are the only time when Jesus is absent in the Gospel narratives, they invite us to enter into our own experience of God's felt absence.

God's absence in our lives is a mystery. God promises to never leave us nor forsake us (Deuteronomy 31:8) and Jesus reiterates that promise (Matthew 28:20), and yet we often experience the haunting sense that God is far away, if not gone completely. Perhaps we know this pain in our relationships, a loved one abandoning us, a cherished friend dying unexpectedly. The loss and absence can be overwhelming and we feel the pain of our aloneness. Our experience of God can feel similar. Imaginative prayer can help us here. We can think of images that evoke our feeling of abandonment—a huge wall between us and God, a vast desert containing nothing but emptiness—that can help us to pray and express our deep loneliness. When we bring these images to prayer, we allow God to hear our hearts and all the emotions that cannot be contained. We join the disciples in their Holy Saturday pain. We join Jesus as he experienced his own forsakenness.

In this next prayer exercise, we will spend time with the disciples on the day after Jesus' death, joining them in their confusion and pain.

IMAGINATIVE PRAYER EXERCISE: PRAYING WITH HOLY SATURDAY (ISAIAH 53 AND PSALM 88)

You are hiding in a room with the rest of the disciples. You are still afraid that you will be recognized and arrested as one of Jesus' followers. You are terrified that they are going to kill all of you. Is this what Jesus meant about taking up your cross—that we should be ready to suffer as he did? You are ashamed of your fear, and as you look around at the others, you wonder what they are feeling. Some of the women come in and tell you that Jesus' body has been placed in a tomb not far from the city, by Joseph of Arimathea and Nicodemus. You are glad they have done this because you

---

1. Significantly, each Gospel writer mentions the burial of Jesus. The early Christians picked up on this and included his burial in the early creeds of the church. For example, the Nicene Creed (381) says: "For our sake he was crucified under Pontius Pilate, he suffered death and was buried."

want Jesus' body to be protected from looters and honored with a proper burial. You wish you had been there to help. You feel a new wave of shame and grief wash over you. You gave everything to follow Jesus, and now he is gone. You thought he would liberate your people from the Romans, but now you are hiding in the dark. You thought he would be glorified as the Messiah of your people, but he died a horrible death, surrounded by criminals. What good is your sacrifice if you end up dying like him?

You look around the room. What do you notice about the others?

As you wrestle with your fear and grief, one of the women begins to sing softly yet mournfully a passage from the prophet Isaiah.

> He was oppressed and afflicted
> yet he did not open his mouth;
> he was led like a lamb to the slaughter
> and as a sheep before her shearers is silent
> so he did not open his mouth . . .
> He was assigned a grave with the wicked,
> and with the rich in his death,
> though he had done no violence
> nor was any deceit in his mouth (Isaiah 53:7, 9).

You and the rest of the disciples begin to weep, crying out to God in pain and anger.

Turn to Psalm 88 and enter into the dark void of these days after the crucifixion, joining the disciples in their grief. Read slowly and imagine the phrases as deeply true of you in your sadness.

> I am overwhelmed with troubles
> and my life draws near to death.
> I am counted among those who go down to the pit;
> I am like one without strength.
> I am set apart with the dead,
> like the slain who lie in the grave,
> whom you remember no more,
> who are cut off from your care . . .
> You have taken from me friend and neighbor—
> darkness is my closest friend.
> (Psalm 88:3–5, 18)[2]

2. This is the only psalm that does not end in some form of gratitude or worship and is therefore appropriate to pray on Holy Saturday.

Allow some silence to enfold you for a few moments before continuing on. Are you being invited to engage with Jesus about your experience of his presence in your life? What images emerge for you as you think about these things? Can you pray them?

PRACTICING RESURRECTION[3]

The darkness slowly begins to fade. Light rises on the horizon. Life has taken on death and won! Jesus is alive!

The mystery at the center of the resurrected life is that it has already happened, we have already "been raised with Christ" (Colossians 3:1). If we love Jesus and are seeking to follow him, then we are already "seated at the right hand of God" and can "set [our] hearts on things above" (Colossians 3:1). But when we look around at the world and our own lives and see all the struggle and pain, worry and fear, we might find it difficult to understand how we have been "raised with Christ."

While this mystery is still unfolding for each of us, we have *already* received the power to live a very different life than we thought possible. As Paul writes in Romans, "If the Spirit of him who raised Jesus from the dead is living in you, he who raised Christ from the dead will also give life to your mortal bodies because of his Spirit who lives in you" (Romans 8:11). The resurrected Jesus, who defeated sin and is living on the far side of death, continues to live within us now by the Holy Spirit. God's *life* is already operative within us, and we are already living *with* God. We do not know where God will lead us, but as Eugene Peterson says, "We live our lives in the practice of what we do not originate and cannot anticipate . . . When we practice resurrection we keep company with Jesus, active and present, who knows where we are going better than we can anticipate."[4] Jesus reminds his friend Martha, and us, "I *am* the resurrection and the life" (John 11:25 emphasis added). Living resurrection is not something we do as much as people we are.

---

3. This phrase taken from Eugene Peterson's book of the same title: *Practicing Resurrection*.

4. Peterson, *Practicing Resurrection*, 8.

LIVING A RESURRECTED LIFE WITH JESUS

Unlike the previous stages of our human relationships, there is no parallel with resurrection. Resurrection is utterly unique. We might have experienced relationships that seem to come back from the dead—a shattered friendship that is restored through forgiveness, an estranged child who returns home, or a broken marriage where love is somehow reborn after divorce papers have been filed. These restorations would feel miraculous in their own way but they still fall short of resurrection. Resurrection implies an entirely new mode of existence, the kind of life we see exemplified in Jesus and explicated in the Sermon on the Mount. A way of life that is impossible for us to live without the presence and power of the Holy Spirit within.

Even though there is no direct equivalent in our human relationships, we can reflect on what a "resurrected life" might look like in these relationships. How might the living Jesus within affect how we interact with and love others? One of the gifts of the imaginative prayer journey is that we have been up close, watching how Jesus engages with people, how he loves and forgives and cares for those around him. We see a human person forgiving people who are harming him, loving people whom others despise, lifting up the dignity of those whom society marginalizes. We see a human being living a life of love before our very eyes.

Dallas Willard was fond of asking, "How would Jesus live your life if he were you?" This is an arresting question. How would Jesus conduct himself as a business person? How would Jesus operate as a bus driver? How would Jesus live a life at home, raising kids? Our prayer journey invites us to lean into these questions in our own lives, asking Jesus to help us see with the eyes of our heart what a resurrected life in my body looks like. As we follow the resurrection journey, we do not simply become nicer, more mature, or more developed. Rather, we are set free from the shackles of death and brought back to life! As we practice living a resurrected life, we will learn how to lay down our lives, to put others' interests ahead of our own, and love in increasingly sacrificial ways.

JESUS COMES TO HIS FRIENDS

The Gospels recount only a few stories about Jesus after the resurrection. Mary encounters Jesus in the Garden (John 20:10–18). Jesus appears to the disciples while they were hiding in the locked room (John 20:19–31).

Later, on the beach in Galilee, Jesus meets the disciples and makes them breakfast (John 21:1–25). In Luke, Jesus appears to two friends on their way to Emmaus (Luke 24). Paul also has a mystical encounter with Jesus as he is walking on the road to Damascus (Acts 9:1–5), and he later writes that Jesus appeared to "more than five hundred of the brothers at the same time" (1 Corinthians 15:6).

As we enter the post-resurrection stories imaginatively, we can make several important observations. First, we notice that Jesus is a *real* person. He is not a ghost or a disembodied spirit. He sits, eats, and talks with his friends. He has a conversation with Mary in the garden. He makes breakfast on the beach for his friends. He walks on a real road and has a real conversation with the two disciples as they walk to Emmaus. Though many have tried to explain away these experiences as group hallucinations or hypnosis, the text is unambiguous that Jesus is a real person. Though he is renewed and transformed, he is still human. And he continues to be interested in cultivating close relationships of love and trust with his friends.

Second, we notice that Jesus' friends do not immediately recognize him. When Mary first speaks to Jesus, she is distraught and grieving. Feeling her loss intently, she is distracted and worried about where Jesus' body has been taken. Mistaking him for a gardener, she beseeches him, saying "Sir, if you have carried him away, tell me where you have put him and I will get him." Then Jesus looks at her and calls her by name. When Mary hears Jesus speak her name, their relationship comes rushing back. Her eyes are opened, and she sees Jesus as her teacher, master, and Lord once again.

Similarly, the friends who are walking to Emmaus think that Jesus is simply a traveling companion. They do not recognize Jesus until they are sitting together at a table and he breaks bread for the meal. In the context of hospitality and friendship, he opens their eyes. He does not reveal himself to Pilate or to the High Priest in order to vindicate himself, but quietly comes to his friends so that they will know he is who he said he was.

When we seek Jesus in imaginative prayer, we may not recognize him either. We may cry out about our deep loss with Mary or express our lost hope with the Emmaus friends. We may not "find" him or "discover" him through our blind, vulnerable, distraught, confused, or angry prayers. Yet, as he hears our hearts yearning for friendship, when the time is right, he opens our eyes and reveals himself as a friend.

We might be relieved that it is not up to us to pray the right way in order to experience the reality of Jesus in our lives, but we may also feel frustrated about our lack of control. We cannot open our own eyes. Jesus will not appear at our command. Our longing for the resurrected Jesus might look more like Mary's fear and despair or the Emmaus friends' confusion and loss of hope than any particular kind of prayer we can muster. We struggle to wait for the Lord, to allow him to come to us in friendship and so we may be tempted to try a different technique in prayer or give up altogether. But these stories reveal Jesus as the one who seeks us out, finding us in our tears, coming alongside us in our confusion. In time, he will open our eyes so we can see him as a friend.

Third, we notice that Jesus meets us in our failure. In chapter 9, we noted both Thomas and Peter fail to follow Jesus to his death. Their fervent determination is extinguished by fear. But Jesus seeks them out and comes to them in love. He does not chastise Thomas for his lack of faith, nor his fear in running away. Rather, he leans toward Thomas and invites him to touch his wounds, put his hands on the scars. In this moment, Thomas is deeply touched, falling to the ground to worship Jesus, saying, "My Lord and my God." (John 20:28).

In John 21, the resurrected Jesus seeks out Peter, who so confidently declared that he would stay with Jesus to the end. After failing miserably, Peter returns to his boat to fish. Jesus stands on the beach and tells Peter and the others to throw the nets on the other side of the boat, a moment that echoes the beginning of their relationship three years earlier.[5] After hauling in a great catch, Peter, recognizing Jesus, throws himself over the side of the boat, and swims to shore. Later, as he and Jesus sit down together over breakfast on the beach, Jesus asks, "Do you love me, Peter?" three times, covering each of Peter's denials with an invitation toward love. In this way, he restores his friendship with Peter.

Finally, we see Jesus physically leaving the disciples so that the Holy Spirit can come to live *within* them. "I will not leave you as orphans," Jesus tells them, "I will come to you" (John 14:18). He promises that the Holy Spirit will reside with them, not as a physical human being who eats, walks, and talks, but as the presence of God living within each of them, drawing them into the love of God.

In the following imaginative prayer exercise, we will pray with Mary Magdalene as she encounters Jesus in the garden outside the tomb on that first Easter morning. You might imagine yourself as Mary, or a friend

---

5. The first story is found in Luke 5:1–11.

accompanying Mary on this early morning sojourn to the tomb of your beloved friend and teacher.

IMAGINATIVE PRAYER EXERCISE: MARY AT THE EMPTY TOMB (JOHN 20:1-18)

You are cold. It is still dark. You have not slept at all, as you have spent the night weeping and groaning for Jesus. You are haunted by the images of him hanging on the cross, gasping for breath. You can still feel the weight of his mother leaning on your arm, shaking. You can still hear the soldiers jeering. You get up and dress. You want to go to the tomb to make burial preparations. You have done this for other family members and want to make sure it is done properly for Jesus.

You walk alone in the darkness to the garden. Though you are exhausted, the walk begins to settle your mind. You hear a night bird chirping and feel an unexpected peace wash over you as you listen to the familiar sound.

When you reach the tomb, you are startled to see the stone pushed away from the entrance. In the pale light of the sunrise you stare at the tomb, wondering if you have come to the right place. All the other tombs are still sealed. You reach out and touch the boulder that has been rolled away. You look this way and that, confused, frightened. Your eyes open wide, you spin around and bolt back to the village.

When you reach the house where your friends are staying, you call out, "They have taken the Lord out of the tomb!" You gasp for breath. "I don't know where they have put him." You hold back your tears.

Peter and John rush past you, knocking over the washing pot by the door. You hike up your skirt and run after them as fast as you can.

When you arrive at the tomb, your heart is pounding. Peter and John look confused and harried. They brush past you, shaking their heads and muttering as they head swiftly back to the village.

You remain, slowly slumping to the ground. Now the tears come. You realize that you won't be able to care for your Master's body. You remain there for several minutes before you decide to look inside. You step cautiously towards the tomb opening and lean in, taking one step, then another.

You draw back suddenly, startled to see two men, dressed all in white, sitting at either end of the long stone slab, the place where Jesus' body should have been. You try to back away but your limbs feel stiff and heavy.

"Woman, why are you crying? One of the men says softly.

"Someone has taken my Lord," you stammer. "Where is he?"

Before they can answer, you sense someone behind you and you spin around. Another man stands there.

"Woman," he says, *"Why are you crying? Who is it you are looking for?"*

The gardener, you think. *Maybe he will know something.*

"Sir, please, if you have carried him away . . ." Your voice breaks. "Please tell me where you have taken him so I can get him."

You look down and turn away. There is a long pause, then,

"Mary," the man says.

That voice! You recognize it instantly. You look up and find his eyes. "Teacher?"

Your heart is pounding. Your whole body feels electric. You reach out to touch him, but he steps back.

"Mary, do not hold on to me, for I have not yet returned to the Father. Go instead to my brothers and tell them this, 'I am returning to my Father and your Father, to my God and your God.'"

You stare at his face. It is *him!*

～

Take some time to absorb everything that you have seen this morning. Are there any questions you would like to ask Jesus? What do you want to tell him? How do you imagine yourself telling the others that you have seen the Lord? How do you imagine them responding? Take time to reflect on this experience before moving on. What is the Spirit revealing about your present life?

LIVING FOR JESUS

Have you ever been rescued or recovered from the brink of death? Those who come near to death—such as prisoners of war—must feel a fulsome thirst for life once rescued. They might imagine how they will live a more meaningful life, appreciate the small things, and spend more time with friends. They must see the world and everything in it with more color, vibrancy, and intensity. Their brush with death makes life that much more valuable.

When we are raised with Christ, we experience this new way of seeing our lives. In Romans 6, Paul says that as followers of Jesus, we have been united with him in his death and therefore will be united with him in his resurrection. Our old selves were prisoners to sin, and we saw God and all of life in a distorted way, but now we have been set free to see God and life in all its vivid, vibrant fullness. When we stand before the cross of Jesus and witness his death and then release our old selves so that we can die *with* him, his resurrection becomes our resurrection. As Paul explains in Romans, "The death he died, he died to sin, once for all, but the life he lives, he lives to God. In the same way, count yourselves dead to sin, but alive to God in Christ Jesus" (Romans 6:10–11). We can now "offer [ourselves] to God, as those who have been brought from death to life" (Romans 6:13). We have moved from living for ourselves to living for Jesus. Our self-centered life has been transformed to a God-centered life.

None of this makes any sense to us who have lived thinking that we must create and sustain our own lives. How can we possibly survive in this world without "looking out for number one"? Jesus has been showing us how. He has been living a life before our eyes that reveals the God-centered life as the only true life. We have watched as Jesus offered forgiveness to those who were killing him. We have seen him offering himself in selfless love to others. Is it possible for us to live like that? When we seek our own security, we follow the way of death and become trapped in the prison of the self. The resurrection beckons us into an entirely new way of living.

A NEW WAY OF LIVING

"Resurrection life . . . is totally different from what we are used to," Eugene Peterson writes, "as different as death is from life."[6] A resurrected life lives off the power and energy of God's liberating grace, a "foundational reorientation from living anxiously by my wits and muscle to living effortlessly in the world of God's active presence."[7] Have you noticed how Jesus models this non-anxious way of living during your imaginative prayer journey? He is never in a rush. He is not looking to secure his future with plans and achievements. He lives fully in the present, following his Father, loving the ones who are right in front of him. He does not need to protect himself

6. Peterson, *Practice Resurrection,* 89.
7. Peterson, *Practice Resurrection,* 96.

from others to secure a sense of self. He models the life we were created to live in his kingdom, free and other-focused.

Jesus not only *describes* the kingdom of God in the Gospels, he *lives* it. After telling his disciples that the weak and the marginalized are first in the kingdom, we see him spending time with lepers, children, and Samaritans. After telling his disciples to "bless those who curse you," he weeps over Jerusalem and those who want him dead. After telling his disciples to love their enemies, he forgives his executioners. As we watch Jesus live a kingdom life before us, we catch a vision for life as it is *meant* it to be lived—and then he invites us to follow him into that resurrected life.

This resurrected life is not about power and position, but service and love. It is not a spiritual accomplishment wrought from our own strength, but a *gift*. Jesus himself waited to be raised by the Father, and he calls us to wait and listen as we seek to follow him in prayer and service, love, and obedience. While spiritual practices and disciplines will be part of our resurrection life, they are not our personal achievements, but ways to help us remain open to the Father. Even though we are raised with Christ, we must continue to "offer ourselves to God," as Paul says, so that he might continue to shape and renew us into the likeness of Jesus.

Yet we cannot simply "try on" a resurrection life. Once we've been brought back to life, we will begin to discover who we were always meant to be. Eugene Peterson reminds us of the completely different nature of this grace-filled resurrection living, using the illustration of running our fingers through water and recognizing that it cannot possibly be strong enough to hold us—until we fall into it. "This living in Jesus—there is no explaining its logic. One must simply let go into it."[8] We have to "let go" to know the reality of being held and sustained in this way.

John ends his Gospel by telling the story of Peter's encounter with the resurrected Jesus (John 21). When Peter meets Jesus on the beach we see a profoundly different man from the Peter we first met in Luke 5, ashamed and afraid to be close to Jesus. Now, in John 21, after three years of being with Jesus and living through the resurrection, Peter cannot wait to get close to him. As you enter into this story you might want to put yourself into Peter's shoes, remembering that, in your own way, you feel you have disappointed Jesus immensely. You have betrayed his friendship and his trust. You are not sure what the future holds.

---

8. Peterson, *Practicing Resurrection*, 96.

IMAGINATIVE PRAYER EXERCISE: ON THE BEACH (JOHN 21)

You're back on your boat, fishing with your friends, but no one has caught anything all night. Your heart just isn't in the work. You've been remembering your final meal with Jesus, how you boasted that you would never leave his side. You wince as you remember all the soldiers, their accusations and taunts, the fear that twisted your gut. You remember seeing Jesus in the courtyard, his bruised and bloodied face, the fire you felt in your cheeks when your eyes met after you said you didn't even know him. The others haven't said anything to you about that night, but you wonder if they know. They *must* know. You feel a lump in your throat as you remember how you hid during the crucifixion with the others, terrified of being found, certain that you had sacrificed three years of your life for nothing. You're finding it difficult to look anyone in the eye.

"Hey. Who's that? Your brother calls out. You look up and squint your eyes. "There," he points, "on the beach." Your heart pounds and your palms sweat.

"You were with him! You're one of his friends," that girl in the courtyard had said, accusingly. Why could I not stand with him? This question haunts and condemns you.

"Throw your nets on the other side of the boat," says the voice from the beach.

You're jolted back to another memory. Three years ago, Jesus said these same words to you when you first met. What a catch that day! Then he invited you into his circle of friends, but you turned away. You felt so unworthy. Yet he still wanted you. "Could he still want me now? After what I've done?" you wonder.

The others in the boat are hauling in fish now. The boat is keeling over, its gunwale dipping beneath the surface of the water. "Help!" the others yell.

"It's the Lord!" John cries out.

Your heart is racing. You have to go to him. You throw off your outer cloak and jump into the water. *Forgive me, Jesus.* You propel your body through the water until you feel your feet touch the bottom. *I was afraid.* You struggle to the shore, your head down, afraid to look in his eyes. *I'll never deny you again.* All your thoughts, your excuses, seem so hollow. You stand before him, waiting.

"Why don't you get some of those fish" he says. "I'm hungry. Let's have breakfast."

You look up and see his laughing eyes.

You run back to the boat, which is close to shore now, and fill a basket with fish. Your hands are shaking as you give him the basket, smiling hesitantly. He cleans the fish quickly and cooks them over a fire while you help the others tie up the boat and sort the fish. When he calls you to eat, you put your work down. Everyone eats hungrily, with little conversation. After the meal, the others go back to sorting fish but you see Jesus looking at you, asking you silently to remain behind. You feel the shame descend on you like a heavy blanket. *Here it comes. What will I say?*

He looks at you, then asks, *"Do you love me, _____?* (Imagine hearing your own name on Jesus' lips).

How do you respond?

He asks again, *"Do you love me, _____?"* He listens to your response.

A third time, he asks, *"Do you love me, _____?* As he looks intently at you, how do you feel stirred to respond?

You turn around and point to your friends at the boat. "What about them?"

"Don't worry about them. You, follow me."

How do you want to respond to Jesus?

As a way to conclude your prayer, you may want to pray this prayer from Ignatius of Loyola:

> *Take, Lord, and receive all my liberty, my memory,*
> *my understanding, and my entire will—*
> *all that I have and call my own.*
> *You have given it all to me. To you, Lord, I return it.*
> *Everything is yours. Do with it what you will.*
> *Give me only your love and grace.*
> *That is enough for me.*[9]

---

9. This is David Fleming's translation of Ignatius' prayer. Fleming, *Draw Me Into Your Friendship,* 177.

Epilogue

Coming Home to Jesus

My eyes are ever on the Lord.

—Psalm 25:15

As a child, I remember looking intently out the car window whenever we returned to our city on our way home from vacation. I kept hoping to see something new, something that had changed since we had left three long weeks before. What had happened while we were away? Was there a new house going up? A new store opening? I would feel a jolt of excitement whenever my eyes landed upon a new structure or a reshaped lot. I was always glad to see any sign that life had continued at home while we were away, that there was something new to investigate, receive, and participate in after my own experience of adventure.

As we conclude our imaginative prayer journey, you may find yourself looking around your own life for signs of something new. When you peruse the landscape of your heart, do you notice new insights, gratitude, or intimacy? Perhaps you feel you have arrived back "home" and see that all is familiar—and yet nothing is the same.

When Jesus speaks to Peter on the beach in John 21, restoring their relationship of love after Peter's denial, his parting words are, "Follow me." This invitation undergirds all that Jesus has said and done. When he first met Peter on the boat he called him to follow. Now, after years of friendship, he repeats the call: "Follow me."

Jesus invites you and I to keep following as well. As we follow him, we will continue to face our emptiness, brokenness, fears, and insecurities, but as we learn to trust and surrender to him—even if the journey leads us to a cross—we will discover that the rhythms of dying and rising are being ingrained in us. Over and over again, we will find ourselves standing before an empty tomb, where he will beckon us with his resurrected body, repeating his invitation to *"Come, follow me."* He will not leave us to fend for ourselves on this life journey. He will live *with* us, and we will begin to discover that as we live with him, he will bring us home to love.

In the course of this book, as you have prayerfully entered the Gospel stories, I hope that your imagination has been given space to breathe, and you have found yourself falling in love with Jesus. For living with Jesus will draw us into a life of continually receiving love and giving love. Love compels us to turn and pay attention to Jesus. Love energizes us to follow him. Love enables us to trust him and surrender to him. To follow Jesus is to live a life of love.

CULTIVATING LONG AND LOVING FRIENDSHIPS

On the night I was fired from my job as a pastor, I returned home stunned, shaken, and deeply broken. I had not seen this coming. I was in shock, mostly, and hardly knew what I felt. We were only home a few minutes when the phone rang. It was our friends Dave and Ariana. They knew we had been at a meeting at church but did not know what it was about. "Dan's been fired," Andrea told them. "We'll be right there!" They dropped everything and sped to our house. At the time they lived several miles away but were there quickly. They felt our need and our pain and rushed straight into it in order to love us.

In many ways this is an ordinary story. We all do this kind of thing when our friends or family are in pain. But we must not let the ordinariness of this experience obscure what is happening—we are engaging in the very stuff of life. We are living lives of love. My friends placed themselves in the middle of my pain that night and offered their presence as a love gift. I can still get emotional thinking about it even though it happened over twenty-five years ago. Being on the receiving end of love is always a powerful experience.

As much as this prayer journey has been a personal and perhaps individual journey, the love of Jesus will always drive us toward others. As our love for Jesus grows, our capacity to love others grows as well. And as we love and serve others, our love for God deepens and expands. We cannot grow in intimacy with Jesus without being led toward others.

Yet our individualistic culture is particularly susceptible to the temptation of thinking only of ourselves. I know that I am. I once imagined myself sitting with Jesus on a riverbank, talking to him about how I was feeling and what was going on in my life. I was feeling uncommonly close to him, cherishing how intently he was listening to me. After a lull in our conversation, I sensed Jesus getting up and walking away. I had never experienced this before so I got up and followed him, assuming that he wanted to show me something. He walked along the riverbank for a while and then, as the river made a turn, Jesus took another path heading down a hill toward a little town. I stopped. I did not want to be with other people. This was *my* time to be with the Lord. But Jesus kept on walking so I caught up to him and started complaining, though I knew I was behaving selfishly by wanting to keep Jesus all to myself.

Undeterred by my complaints, Jesus kept walking, and I had to hurry to keep up with him. As we entered the town, Jesus approached a merchant who was setting up a fruit stand and began talking to him. I stood back, hoping this would be over soon.

Then Jesus turned and said to me, "Dan, come and meet my friend Ben." I hesitated, but eventually walked over and greeted Ben.

I felt convicted but loved that day. Jesus did not want me to spend time with him in order to keep him to myself. He has many friends, and he wants all of us to live in love *with* him and *with* each other. As this imaginative prayer experience revealed to me, we cannot develop a friendship with Jesus without also building friendships with others.

Throughout our prayer journey, we have seen how developing a relationship with Jesus takes time and work—and this is also true in our friendships with others. We need to prioritize the cultivation of friendships in our life. Imaginative prayer often stirs up our desire for the comforting presence of Jesus, and he usually offers this through the loving and patient presence of friends.

THE JOURNEY HOME

As we "come home" from our prayer journey, you may feel that your journey has just begun! Any time I have a new experience of God, or a fresh encounter with "life from above" (John 3:3), I often feel as if I am beginning my life with Jesus for the first time. Such is the reality of God's love; always new, always expanding. And always transforming. Praying with the stories of Jesus, contemplating his presence, works in us over time to transform us more and more into his likeness. We become like the one whom we contemplate.[1]

Several years ago, a local TV ad campaign ran pictures of dogs with their owners while pitching a product. In every ad, there was a striking and comical resemblance between the dogs and their owners. As we live in close proximity with others, we slowly begin to look like each other. We take on each other's mannerisms, say the same phrases, express similar attitudes. Over time, we become similar to those with whom we share life. In this same way, the more time we spend living *with* Jesus in our prayerful imagination, watching him, listening to him, and following him, the more we will become like him. As we live with Jesus, we will be transformed by him. Our life with Jesus is a *transformational* journey, where we move from being strangers of God to friends with God, from knowledge of Jesus to a deeper experience of Jesus. Living with Jesus will involve a lifetime of change, a lifetime of yielding to the transforming work of the Spirit, who conforms us to the image of Jesus. Through prayer, we engage with God and we say, "Yes," to his transforming work within us. Through prayer, we rest in the presence and love of Jesus and nurture our friendship with him.

Jesus not only rescues us from self-destruction but also fulfills our heart's deepest longing, which is to love and to be loved. Yet we so quickly focus on our behavior, our need to practice spiritual disciples, and whether or not our theology is correct. The core of our life is Jesus. When God speaks to us, he is not primarily interested in giving us instructions. He wants to give us his own self in the person of Jesus. As we journey home, let us continue to "fix our eyes on Jesus" (Hebrews 12:2).

This final exercise in our imaginative prayer journey is not taken from Scripture but is based on an experience I had while listening to an instructor lead a class discussion about growing in friendship with Jesus. May the Lord meet you in this imagined scene through the particular details of your own life.

---

1. The phrase is taken from George Aschenbrenner's article of the same name.

IMAGINATIVE PRAYER EXERCISE: COMING HOME

I don't know how, but I am aware that I have died and am waiting somewhere that is neither cold nor warm, but "in between." There are others waiting here with me. We smile at one another though I do not recognize anyone.

When I hear a call come, I know that we are being summoned to meet Jesus. This awareness simply appears in my mind. My heart beats a little faster as we rise and begin to move.

As we walk, the space around us is getting lighter and warmer. Someone asks their neighbor, "What are you going to say?" This question lodges itself in my mind. What *will* I say? I have thought about this so much in my life. I have prayed so many prayers, filled so many journals with questions and wonderings, words of gratitude, anger, love, grief, confession, sorrow, repentance, and lament to God. What will I say *now* that I am actually face to face with him?

I slow my pace as I rehearse this conversation. There are many things that I want to bring into the light, and I want to be as open and honest as I can. I think I should begin with confession. I feel the shame rise within me as I reckon with all the ways I have failed to trust and obey him. I also feel the resistance rising up within me, but I know I need to trust his mercy, trust that he will accept me. I remember his promise that he receives the broken-hearted and will not snuff out a bruised reed.

After my confession, I imagine myself admitting all the things I got wrong about God, the ways I misunderstood him, the tensions I constantly lived in between justice and mercy, holiness and love, obedience and grace. My anxiety about these tensions and all that I have gotten wrong begin to fade as I become increasingly aware of the brightness before me. It is a warm light, sharp and real. It draws me forward. I am walking, but I am aware that the mysterious power compelling me forward is joy.

As we come around a bend, I think I see . . . *him.*

In the light of his brightness, warmth, and joy, everything else fades. I see him watching me, his eyes drawing me to come closer to him. My heart races. My mind spins.

All around him, people are radiating light and laughter and buoyancy. I see him lean toward someone on his left, his eyes bright with recognition, and I hear him say,

"Look! Here comes my friend, Dan!"

FOR GROUP STUDY

Please visit www.danheavenor.com to find downloadable study questions for each chapter of the book to use with a group as well as audio versions of the prayer exercises in this book.

ABOUT THE AUTHOR

Dan Heavenor is a spiritual director and bus driver living in North Vancouver, British Columbia. He has been offering spiritual direction and leading prayer retreats for over twenty years. He has also been driving a bus for the city of Vancouver for over twenty-five years. A former pastor, Dan now offers individual spiritual direction, as well as leading weekend retreats on spirituality and prayer. His passion and calling is to walk with others as they seek after God, ask their questions, and live their journey with God in all its complexity and uniqueness. Dan received his Doctor of Ministry degree in imaginative prayer and Ignatian spirituality at Carey Theological College and his MDiv from Regent College, Vancouver. He is married to Andrea and they have four adult children, three "children-in-law" and three beautiful grandkids.

To contact Dan to speak at your gathering or lead weekend retreats, please contact him at www.danheavenor.com.

Bibliography

Aelred of Rievaulx. *Spiritual Friendship.* Kalamazoo, MI: Cistercian, 1977.

Aschenbrenner, George. "Becoming Whom We Contemplate." *The Way Supplement* 52 (1985) 30–42.

Barry, William A., and William J. Connolly. *The Practice of Spiritual Direction.* San Francisco: Harper and Row, 1982.

Benner, David. *Surrender to Love.* Downers Grove, IL: InterVarsity, 2003.

Bonhoeffer, Deitrich. *The Cost of Discipleship.* New York: MacMillan, 1980.

———. *God Is in the Manger.* Louisville, KY: Westminster John Knox, 2012.

Casey, Michael. *Toward God: The Ancient Wisdom of Western Prayer.* Liguori, MO: Liguori, 1996.

Crossroads Initiative Website. "Prayer of Abandonment–Charles De Foucauld." Accessed Feb 20, 2024. https://www.crossroadsinitiative.com/media/articles/prayer-of-abandonment-charles-de-foucauld/.

Culp, A.J., and Dru Johnson. "A.J. Culp—Memoirs of Moses." *OnScript.* Podcast, MP3. 1:09:01. Sept 29, 2020. https://onscript.study/podcast/a-j-culp-memoir-of-moses/.

Doidge, Norman. *The Brain that Changes Itself: Stories of Personal Triumph from the Frontiers of Brain Science.* New York: Viking, 2007.

Edgar, Brian. *The God Who Plays: A Playful Approach to Theology and Spirituality.* Eugene, OR: Cascade, 2017.

Egan, Robert. "Jesus in the Heart's Imagination." *The Way Supplement* 84 (1995) 62–71.

Finley, James. *The Awakening Call.* Notre Dame, IN: Ave Maria, 1984.

Fischer, Kathleen. *The Inner Rainbow.* New York: Paulist, 1983.

Fitzgerald, Kathryn. "The Central Role of Imagination in Effecting Spiritual Transformation," DMin diss., Lancaster Theological Seminary, 1998.

Fleming, David L, S.J., *Draw Me Into Your Friendship.* St Louis, MO: Institute of Jesuit Sources, 1996.

Foster, Richard. *Prayer.* New York: HarperSanFrancisco, 1992.

Hart, Trevor Hart. *Between the Image and the Word.* Burlington, VT: Ashgate, 2013.

Kelsey, Morton. *The Other Side of Silence.* New York: Paulist, 1976.

Lewis, C.S. *Mere Christianity.* New York: MacMillan, 1943.

McIntyre, John. *Faith Theology and Imagination.* Edinburgh: Handbell, 1987.

Merton, Thomas. *Contemplative Prayer.* Garden City, NY: Image, 1971.

———. *Wisdom of the Desert.* New York: New Directions, 1970

Nouwen, Henri J.M., with Michael J. Christensen and Rebecca J. Laird. *Spiritual Direction: Wisdom for the Long Walk of Faith.* New York: HarperOne, 2006.

Nouwen, Henri J.M., and Robert A. Jonas. "Henri Nouwen Writings." *Spirituality and Practice* (website). Accessed Feb 20, 2024. https://www.spiritualityandpractice.com/book-reviews/excerpts/view/17109.

Patton, John. *From Ministry to Theology: Pastoral Action and Reflection*. Eugene, OR: Wipf & Stock, 1995.

Parker, Cyndi. *Encountering Jesus in the Real World of the Gospels*. Peabody, MA: Hendrickson, 2021.

Peterson, Eugene. *The Jesus Way*. Grand Rapids, MI: Eerdmans, 2007.

———. *Practicing Resurrection*. Grand Rapids, MI: Eerdmans, 2010.

Rolheiser, Ronald. *The Shattered Lantern: Rediscovering a Felt Presence of God*. London: Holder and Stoughton, 1994.

Rutledge, Fleming. *The Crucifixion*. Grand Rapids, MI: Eerdmans, 2017.

Sanders, Fred. "Thomas Aquinas' Big Pile of Straw." *Scriptorium Daily*. December 6, 2010. https://scriptoriumdaily.com/thomas-aquinas-big-pile-of-straw/.

Sheldrake, Philip. "Imagination and Prayer." *The Way* 24 (1984) 92–102.

Smith, James K.A. *Imagining the Kingdom*. Grand Rapids, MI: Baker, 2013.

———. *You Are What You Love*. Grand Rapids, MI: Brazos, 2016.

Taylor, Joan. "What Did Jesus Really Look Like?" *BBC*. December 24, 2015. https://www.bbc.com/news/magazine-35120965.

Tozer, A.W. *The Pursuit of God*. Camp Hill, PA: Christian Publications, 1982.

Ulanov, Ann Belford. *Picturing God*. Eugene, OR: Wipf & Stock, 2002.

UMass Chan Medical School Psychiatry Dept. "The 'Still Face' Experiment." July 11, 2022. YouTube video. 01:54. https://www.youtube.com/watch?v=FaiXi8KyzOQ.

von Balthasar, Hans Urs. *Prayer*. San Francisco: Ignatius, 1986.

Whelan, Joseph. "Contemplating Christ." *The Way* 10 (1970) 196–98.

Wilson, Jonathan R. *God's Good World*. Grand Rapids, MI: Baker Academic, 2013.

Zimmerman, Jens. "Abandoning Earth: Personhood and the Techno-Fiction of Transhumanism." *Regent World* 31. 1 (April 28, 2020).

Zodhiates, Spiros. "1690. embromaomai." In *The Complete Word Study Dictionary New Testament*, 574. Chattanooga, TN: AMG, 1992.

www.ingramcontent.com/pod-product-compliance
Lightning Source LLC
Chambersburg PA
CBHW071915160426
42812CB00097B/1107